FIFTY YEARS OF
MODERN VERSE

FIFTY YEARS OF MODERN VERSE

An Anthology

CHOSEN BY

JOHN GAWSWORTH

SECOND PRINTING

London

The Richards Press Ltd.

8 Charles Street, St. James's Square

First published 1938
Reprinted 1949

Printed by Lowe & Brydone Printers Ltd., London, N.W.10

FOR
ERICA

Here I will build a citadel of love
Impregnable against the hours' assault,
So steadfast-rooted in felicity
Its very blemishes possess not fault ;
So garrisoned, so bastioned and secure,
That, placed in loneliness upon a height,
No threatenings may disturb its peace by day,
No scaling foes encroach on it by night.

Life shall dictate its form and Life its mould,
Its towers and keep, its courts, its whole design,
That, when 'tis builded, she for whom I wrought
May cry, " 'Tis Love's own fortress—and 'tis mine ! "

J. G.

Preface

EVEN if there were no limit to the size of this volume, to represent all the best poets publishing since 1888 would be an ambition for the infallible.

Mr. Lennox Robinson has declared that "an anthology of poems is the only kind of book for which no apology need ever be offered"; and I need only add that there is here intended an anthology of poems, and not a comprehensive anthology of poetic reputations. Sixty good, and a handful of great poets, therefore, were listed for omission at the outset, on the ground that familiar examples of their work already filled a large part of every existing collection formed to represent the period of the last fifty years either in whole or in part.

This present selection is, consequently, the product of a wide and diligent search, which demanded the examination of nearly one thousand books. Its purpose has been, in the main, to focus attention on the work of a number of modern writers, Celtic as well as English, whose merits have tended to become obscured in an age when much verse had been produced for a comparatively small audience.

Mr. W. B. Yeats tried, with the one hundred contributors admitted to *The Oxford Book of*

[7]

Preface

Modern Verse, to include "all good poets who have lived or died from three years before the death of Tennyson" until September, 1936. This book attempts, merely, after a fresh survey, to draw attention to the work of some additional writers of the same period.

JOHN GAWSWORTH.

Acknowledgments

THE Editor repeats his grateful acknowledgments for the contributions that appeared in this book in its original form, *Known Signatures* : to Mr. Edmund Blunden and the Twyn Barlwm Press and the Ulysses Press ; to Mr. A. E. Coppard and the Ulysses Press ; to Mr. W. H. Davies and the Twyn Barlwm Press ; to Lord Alfred Douglas ; to the Executors of Ernest Dowson, and to Mr. Desmond Flower ; to Mr. John Drinkwater (and now to his Executors) ; to Mrs. John Freeman ; to Canon John Gray (and now to his Executors) ; to Mr. Hugh MacDiarmid and Messrs. Ernest Benn ; to Mrs. Alida Monro ; to Mr. Herbert Palmer and the Twyn Barlwm Press ; to Miss Edith Sitwell and the Twyn Barlwm Press ; to Mr. L. A. G. Strong ; to Mrs. Edward Thomas and Messrs. Ingpen and Grant.

He further thanks Lord Alfred Douglas for two additional poems from *Sonnets* and *Lyrics* (Rich and Cowan) ; Mr. Maurice Wollman for selecting three substitute poems from *Poems by John Gawsworth* (Richards Press) ; Mr. Wilfrid Gibson for two substitute poems from *Collected Poems* (Macmillan) and *The Golden Room* (Macmillan); the Executors of Lionel Johnson for two substitute uncollected poems ; Mr. Hugh MacDiarmid for two additional poems from *Selected Poems* (Macmillan) and two additional poems from *Stony Limits* (Gollancz) ; Mr. Thomas P. Middleton and Mr. Henry Savage for two substitute poems to represent Richard Middleton, from *Twenty-Five New Poems*

Acknowledgments

(Richards Press) and John Gawsworth's *The Poets of Merchant Taylors' School* (Rich and Cowan); Mr. Herbert Palmer for a substitute poem from *Neo-Georgian Poetry : 1936-1937* (Richards Press); and Mrs. Ada Wratislaw for two substitute poems to represent Theodore Wratislaw, from *Selected Poems* (Richards Press).

For the poems augmenting the book in this edition, he desires to express his sincere gratitude to the following poets, legal representatives and publishers :

Lord Tenterden for a poem from *Prose Pieces and Poems* by the Hon Anthony Abbott (Gollancz);

Prof. Lascelles Abercrombie for a poem from *Interludes and Poems* (Lane : The Bodley Head);

Mr. J. Redwood Anderson for a poem from *Haunted Islands : Part One* (Blackwell);

Miss Marion Angus for two poems from *The Turn of the Day* (Porpoise Press : Faber and Faber);

The Executors of F. W. Bourdillon for a poem from *Moth-Wings* (Mathews);

The Executors of D. J. O'Donoghue for two poems from *Poems* by Thomas Boyd (O'Donoghue);

Mr. F. V. Branford for a poem from *Titans and Gods* (Christophers);

Mr. Gerald Bullett for a poem from *Poems in Pencil* (Dent);

Mr. Seumas MacManus for a poem from *The Four Winds of Eirinn* by Ethna Carbery (Gill);

Mr. W. H. Chesson for five poems from *Selected Poems* by Nora Hopper Chesson (Rivers);

Mr. Wilfred Rowland Childe for four poems from *Selected Poems* (Nelson) and for two poems from *Neo-Georgian Poetry : 1936-1937* (Richards Press);

Mrs. Frances Cornford for a poem from *Different Days* (Hogarth Press);

Mrs. Charlotte Crawford for a poem from *In Quiet Fields* by Robert Crawford (Porpoise Press : Faber and Faber);

Mrs. Nina Cust for a poem from *Occasional Poems* by Henry Cust (Jerusalem : Privately Printed);

Acknowledgments

Prof. W. MacNeile Dixon for a poem from *In Arcadia* (Blackie) and for one from John Cooke's *The Dublin Book of Irish Verse* (Hodges, Figgis);

Prof. E. R. Dodds for a poem from *Thirty-two Poems* (Constable);

Mr. John Eglinton for a poem from Padric Gregory's *Modern Anglo-Irish Verse* (Nutt);

Mr. Havelock Ellis for a poem from *Poems* (Richards Press);

Mr. T. Sturge Moore for three poems from *A Selection from the Poems of Michael Field* (Poetry Bookshop);

Miss Alice Furlong for a poem from Padric Gregory's *Modern Anglo-Irish Verse* (Nutt);

Mr. Monk Gibbon for a poem from *For Daws to Peck At* (Gollancz);

Miss Stella Gibbons for a poem from *The Mountain Beast* (Longmans, Green);

Dr. Oliver St. J. Gogarty for two poems from *Others to Adorn* (Rich and Cowan);

Mr. Douglas Goldring for a poem from *Streets* (Selwyn and Blount) and one from *Odd Man Out* (Chapman and Hall);

Miss Esther Roper for a poem from *The Poems of Eva Gore-Booth* (Longmans, Green);

Dr. Philip Gosse for a poem from *The Collected Poems of Edmund Gosse* (Heinemann);

Mrs. Ayrton Gould for four poems from *The Collected Poems of Gerald Gould* (Gollancz);

Dr. Alexander Gray for a poem from *Any Man's Life* (Blackwell);

Lady Desborough for two poems by the Hon. Julian Grenfell from *Soldier Poets* (Erskine MacDonald);

Mr. George Rostrevor Hamilton for a poem from *Stars and Fishes* (Lane: The Bodley Head);

Mr. Kenneth Hare for a poem from *The Raven and the Swallow* (Holywell Press) and one from *New Poems* (Benn);

Mr. F. R. Higgins for a poem from *The Dublin Magazine*;

Mrs. Penelope Hodgson for a poem from *Verse and Prose in Peace and War* by W. N. Hodgson (Murray);

The Executors of Herbert P. Horne for four poems from *Diversi Colores* (Chiswick Press) and one from *The Dial: Number Two* (Vale Press);

Acknowledgments

The Executors of A. E. Housman for a poem from *A Shropshire Lad* (Richards Press) and one from *Last Poems* (Richards Press);

Dr. Hyde, President of Eire, for two poems from *Love Songs of Connacht* (Unwin) and one from W. B. Yeats' *A Book of Irish Verse* (Methuen);

Mrs. Janet Image for two poems from *Poems and Carols* (Mathews);

Mr. Fytton Armstrong for a poem from *Memories of a Victorian* by Edgar Jepson (Gollancz);

Mr. Patrick Kavanagh for two uncollected poems and one from *The Dublin Magazine*;

The Hon. Kathleen Lawless for three poems from *With the Wild Geese* by the Hon. Emily Lawless (Isbister);

Mrs. Sylvia Lynd for a poem from *The Yellow Placard* (Gollancz);

Mr. S. R. Lysaght for a poem from *Poems* (Macmillan);

Mr. Arthur Machen for two poems from *The Secret Glory* (Secker and Warburg);

Lt.-Cdr. Hamish Maclaren for two poems from *Sailor with Banjo* (Gollancz) and four from *Neo-Georgian Poetry: 1936-1937* (Richards Press);

Mr. Edward Powys Mathers for a poem from *Coloured Stars* (Blackwell);

Miss N. K. McCausland for two poems from *The Legendary Shore* (Richards Press);

Mrs. Phyllis Mégroz for a poem from *The Silver Bride* (Selwyn and Blount) and one from *The New English Weekly*;

Mr. R. L. Mégroz for a poem from *From the Scrip of Eros* (Fenland Press) and one from *The New English Weekly*;

Mr. E. H. W. Meyerstein for a poem from *In Merlin's Wood* (Blackwell), one from *Selected Poems* (Macmillan), and one from *Edwardian Poetry: 1936* (Richards Press);

Mr. Wilfrid Meynell for two poems from *The Poems of Alice Meynell* (Burns Oates and Washbourne);

Miss Viola Meynell for two poems from *The Frozen Ocean* (Secker);

Miss Susan Miles for a poem from *The Hares* (Mathews);

Miss Alice Milligan for five poems from *Hero Lays* (Maunsel) and for one from *The Book of Saint Ultan* (Lester);

Acknowledgments

Miss Jane G. Mitchell for a poem by Susan L. Mitchell from Grace Rhys' *A Celtic Anthology* (Harrap);

Mr. T. Sturge Moore for three uncollected poems from *The Venture: 1905, The Book of the Poets' Club: 1911* and *The London Mercury*;

Mr. Thomas Moult for a poem from W. H. Davies' *Shorter Lyrics of the Twentieth Century* (Poetry Bookshop);

Mr. Seumas O'Sullivan for three poems from *Poems* (Maunsel) and one from *The Irish Times*;

Mr. Eden Phillpotts for a poem from *Wild Fruit* (Lane: The Bodley Head), four from *Cherry-Stones* (Richards Press) and one from *A Hundred Lyrics* (Benn);

Miss Ruth Pitter for six poems from *First and Second Poems* (Sheed and Ward);

Mr. Max Plowman for a poem from *The Golden Heresy* (Privately Printed);

Sir Arthur Quiller-Couch for a poem from *Poems and Ballads* (Methuen);

Mr. T. W. Ramsey for two poems from *Antares* (Macmillan);

Mr. Ernest Rhys for a poem from *A London Rose* (Mathews and Lane);

Miss Caron Rock for a poem from *Or in the Grass* (Wilson);

Mrs. Maud Rolleston for a poem from *Sea Spray* by T. W. Rolleston (Maunsel);

Miss Ethel Rolt-Wheeler for a poem from *Selected Poems* (Richards Press);

Lady Margaret Sackville for a poem from Bertram Lloyd's *Poems Written During the Great War* (Allen and Unwin);

The Hon. V. Sackville West for a poem from *Collected Poems: Volume One* (Hogarth Press);

Mr. Siegfried Sassoon for a poem from *The Heart's Journey* (Heinemann);

Mr. Michael Scot for a poem from *Neo-Georgian Poetry: 1936-1937* (Richards Press);

Mr. M. P. Shiel for a poem from *Poems* (Richards Press);

Mr. Horace Shipp for a poem from *Hecuba in Camden Town* (Bloomsbury Press) and one from *Palimpsest* (Sampson Low, Marston);

Mr. Lewis Spence for a poem from *The Plumes of Time* (Allen and Unwin);

Mr. Edward Storer for a poem from *Mirrors of Illusion* (Sisley's);

[13]

Acknowledgments

Miss Muriel Stuart for two poems from *Selected Poems* (Cape);

Mr. Arthur Symons for two poems from *Jezebel Mort* (Heinemann);

Mrs. Rachel Annand Taylor for three poems from *The End of Fiametta* (Richards Press);

Mr. A. S. J. Tessimond for a poem from *Edwardian Poetry: 1936* (Richards Press) and one from *Neo-Georgian Poetry: 1936-1937* (Richards Press);

Mr. Wilfrid Meynell for three poems from *The Poetical Works of Francis Thompson* (Burns Oates and Washbourne);

Mr. Wilfrid Thorley for a poem from *The Londoner's Chariot* and one from L. A. G. Strong's *The Best Poems of 1924* (Small, Maynard);

Miss Pamela Travers for a poem from Alida Monro's *Recent Poetry: 1923-1933*, and two from *The New English Weekly*;

Mr. W. J. Turner for a poem from *New Poems* (Chatto and Windus);

Miss Evelyn Underhill for a poem from *Immanence* (Dent);

Prof. Sherard Vines for a poem from *The Pyramid* (Cobden-Sanderson);

Mr. E. H. Visiak for a poem from *Selected Poems* (Richards Press);

Mr. Charles Weekes for two poems from *Reflections and Refractions* (Unwin) and four from *About Women* (Maunsel);

Lady Gerald Wellesley for a poem from *Poems of Ten Years* (Macmillan);

Miss Anna Wickham for a poem from *The Man with a Hammer* (Grant Richards), four poems from *Thirty-six New Poems* (Richards Press) and one uncollected;

Mrs. Margaret L. Woods for two poems from *Collected Poems* (Lane: The Bodley Head);

The Rev. Andrew Young for poem from *Collected Poems* (Cape);

Miss Ella Young for a poem from A. P. Graves' *The Book of Irish Poetry* (Unwin).

A tribute is also due to Miss H. A. Beecham for able assistance.

J. G.

FIFTY YEARS OF
MODERN VERSE

The Hon. *Anthony Abbott*
(1909–1928)

DELIVER ME FROM THE PAIN OF LOVING DAPHNIS

DELIVER me from the pain of loving Daphnis,
Then will I bring thee broad, sweet boughs of
    may,
And myrtle twine around thy golden images.
Deliver me from casting sidelong glances upon
    sweet Daphnis,
Lest ivory curls I kiss, and stumble about his
    white and lovely feet.
If I bestrew large apples from my scrip,
And flute a long and saddened pastoral melody,
Deliver me from the pain of loving Daphnis.

The high and limpid fountains trickle in the
    breeze,
The bushes hum with scents and yellow liquid
    bees
Far down in yonder groves, the woods are
    brushed by deer;
Deliver me, O gods, from the pain of loving
    Daphnis.

My breasts are warmed by the sun's awakened
    passion,
My limbs are carved amid the purple flowers,

[17]

I can scarce hold my breath for pain and sad
  desire,
Lest I behold the magic flute and eyes of Daphnis.
I will offer thee rich cheese, and milk, and jars
  of honey,
Bring figs and vine-leaves round thy shrines and
  wells,
If thou can'st stir the heart of lovely Daphnis
To trample me like daffodils and pale narcissi.

Lascelles Abercrombie

(1881–1938)

ALL LAST NIGHT

ALL last night I was quiet
  In a dream fragrant and warm :
She had become my Sabbath,
  And round my neck, her arm.

I knew the warmth in my dreaming ;
  The fragrance, I suppose,
Was her hair about me,
  Or else she wore a rose.

[18]

Her hair, I think; for likest
 Woodruffe 'twas, when Spring
Loitering down wet woodways
 Treads it sauntering.

No light, nor any speaking;
 Fragrant only and warm.
Enough to know my lodging,
 The white Sabbath of her arm.

J. Redwood Anderson
(1883–   )

THE SEAGULL

THE very spirit of the coast is he.

Precipitous, the high
Cliffs shoot into the sea:
Precipitous, the high cliffs sweep
Into the deep
And green reflection of the sky.

He moves on wings that curve
Like sickles keen and white,

J. Redwood Anderson

Sickles that reap
The azure harvests of the light;
He moves on wings that sleep,
Quivering against the wind that drives;
He moves on wings that suddenly
Slant and swerve
As his white body
Dives.

And all the while, from dawn to night,
And through the night till dawn,
Comes his sharp, melancholy cry
Flung to and fro in flight:
The echo of the name men call him by—
" Fuileán."*

* Pronounced "fweelawn."

Marion Angus
(1870–1946)

ALAS! POOR QUEEN

She was skilled in music and the dance
And the old arts of love,
At the court of the poisoned rose
And the perfumed glove,
And gave her beautiful hand
To the pale Dauphin
A triple crown to win—
And she loved little dogs
    And parrots
      And red-legged partridges
And the golden fishes of the Duc de Guise
And a pigeon with a blue ruff
She had from Monsieur d'Elbœuf.

Master John Knox was no friend to her;
She spoke him soft and kind,
Her honeyed words were Satan's lure
The unwary soul to bind.
" Good sir, doth a lissom shape
And a comely face
Offend your God His Grace
Whose Wisdom maketh these
Golden fishes of the Duc de Guise ? "

She rode through Liddesdale with a song;
" Ye streams sae wondrous strang,
Oh, mak' me a wrack as I come back
But spare me as I gang ! "
While a hill-bird cried and cried
Like a spirit lost
By the grey storm-wind tost.

Consider the way she had to go.
Think of the hungry snare,
The net she herself had woven,
Aware or unaware,
Of the dancing feet grown still,
The blinded eyes.—
Queens should be cold and wise,
And she loved little things,
    Parrots
      And red-legged partridges
And the golden fishes of the Duc de Guise
And the pigeon with the blue ruff
She had from Monsieur d'Elbœuf.

MARY'S SONG

I WAD hae gien him my lips tae kiss
Had I been his, had I been his ;
Barley breid and elder wine,
Had I been his as he is mine.

Marion Angus

The wanderin' bee it seeks the rose;
Tae the lochan's bosom the burnie goes;
The grey bird cries at even' fa',
" My luve, my fair one, come awa!"

My beloved sall hae this hert tae break,
Reid, reid wine and the barley cake,
A hert tae break, and a mou' tae kiss,
Tho' he be nae mine, as I am his.

Edmund Blunden
(1896–   )

THE WEATHERCOCK
(*Flanders*, 1917)

THE turret's leaden carapace
  Is shining coldly in the moon,
  And the winds are in a swoon.
And sad and tarnished, into space,
Pinnacled in the highest place,
  The little golden boy forlorn
  Blows on his hunting-horn.

Call as you may, call as you may,
   You little airy forester,
   The winds will yet demur.
And the harried ghosts may saunter and stray
Untroubled with the swelling bay
   Of the straining hounds of the wind-god, till
   The red sun climbs the smoking hill.

The air's intense with iron frost;
   And you are fettered, golden boy,
   Nor spin in mad-heart joy.
But even now the die is tossed
That bids the winter yield his power,
And soon again upon your tower,
You'll trumpet through the raining night
   The wind's delight,
   The ghost's affright,
The roistering hunter-gale's delight.

IN SUMMER
The Rotunda of the Bishop of Derry

Out of the sparkling flood of green that sways
   and sings to the summer gale,
With many a nautilus afloat of scarlet poppy
   and marguerite,
   Up like a crystal cave
   Above the laughing wave

Arises proud the mansion of a genius none is
      heard to hail,
From whose fantastic sight of truth and beauty
      grew the scene complete.

His sense was delicate; that green, in glassy
      pane, once glanced at sea,
That cold gray mentions fog and crag and
      winter on a coast I dreamed,
    And yet the field and wood
    By most are understood
As far inland, the natural home of heifer, butter-
      cup, and bee;
Here but for him the sun for gardeners, farmers,
      lovers alone had beamed.

By him illusion's island rose, and round a fairy
      ocean flowed,
That dove's long mourning changed into a bell
      that tolls beneath the tide,
    And winged seeds' bright play
    Are as the pearly spray;
And like a riddle lives his presence high above
      the country road,
A spirit of wonder in isolation, unacknowledged,
      satisfied.

Francis William Bourdillon
(1852–1921)

THE NIGHT HAS A THOUSAND EYES

THE night has a thousand eyes,
　　And the day but one;
Yet the light of the bright world dies
　　With the dying sun.

The mind has a thousand eyes,
　　And the heart but one;
Yet the light of a whole life dies
　　When love is done.

Thomas Boyd
(1867–　　)

THE KING'S SON

WHO rideth through the driving rain
　　At such a headlong speed?
Naked and pale he rides amain
　　Upon a naked steed.

Nor hollow nor height his going bars,
　　His wet steed shines like silk,
His head is golden to the stars
　　And his limbs are white as milk.

But, lo, he dwindles as a light
    That lifts from a black mere,
And, as the fair youth wanes from sight,
    The steed grows mightier.

What wizard by yon holy tree
    Mutters unto the sky
Where Macha's flame-tongued horses flee
    On hooves of thunder by?

Ah, 'tis not holy so to ban
    The youth of kingly seed:
Ah! woe, the wasting of a man
    Who changes to a steed.

Nightly upon the Plain of Kings
    When Macha's day is nigh
He gallops; and the dark wind brings
    His lonely human cry.

TO THE LEANAN SIDHE*

WHERE is thy lovely perilous abode?
    In what strange phantom land
Glimmer the faerie turrets whereto rode
    The ill-starred poet band?

* The Fairy Muse

Say, in the Isle of Youth haſt thou thy home,
   The sweeteſt singer there,
Stealing on wingèd ſteed across the foam
   Thorough the moonlit air,

And by the gloomy peak of Errigal,
   Haunted by ſtorm and cloud,
Wing paſt, and to thy lover there let fall
   His singing robe . . . and shroud?

Or, where the miſts of bluebell float beneath
   The red ſtems of the pine
And sunbeams ſtrike through shadows, doſt
    thou breathe
   The word that makes him thine?

Or, is thy palace entered through some cliff
   When radiant tides are full
And round thy lover's wandering ſtarlit skiff
   Coil in luxurious lull?

And, would he, entering on the brimming flood,
   See caverns vast in height,
And diamond columns crowned with leaf and
    bud,
   Glow in long lanes of light,

And there, the pearl of that great glittering shell,
   Trembling behold thee lone,
Now weaving in slow dance an awful spell,
   Now still upon thy throne?

Thy beauty! ah, the eyes that pierce him through
   Then melt into a dream.
The voice that sings the mysteries of the blue
   And all that Be and Seem!

Thy lovely motions answering to the rime
   That ancient Nature sings,
That keeps the stars in cadence for all time
   And echoes through all things.

Whether he sees thee thus, or in his dreams
   Thy light makes all lights dim:
An aching solitude from henceforth seems
   The world of men to him.

Thy luring song, above the sensuous roar,
   He follows with delight
Shutting behind him Life's last gloomy door
   And fares into the Night.

F. V. Branford
(1894–1941)

MAN

HE walks the world with mountains in his
    breast,
And holds the hiltless wind in vassalage.
Transtellar spaces are his fields of quest,
Eternity his spirit's ambassage.
The uneared acre of the firmaments
Under his hungry harrow, yields increase.
While, from the threshold of dim continents
They beckon him, who bear the stars in lease.

And yet is he a thane of foreigners,
On sapphire throned, but in an unkinged house,
Arrased with honours, broidered in gold
    sheen—
A palace in a town of sepulchres.
Voices he hears, but knows not what they mean,
His own to him the most mysterious.

Gerald Bullett
(1893–)

THE LOVER BIDS HIS HEART BE ABSENT

BECAUSE I love her,
The sky is dark above her.
Because I find her fair,
There is a menace in the very air.
A single leaf of the tree
Is not more frail than she,
Whose every breath
Draws her, because I love her, nearer death.
So, heart, absent you from me now, that I,
Lest the belovèd die,
May feign I do not love her.

Ethna Carbery
(1873–1901)

THE LOVE-TALKER

I MET the Love-Talker one eve in the glen,
He was handsomer than any of our handsome
    young men.
His eyes were blacker than the sloe, his voice
    sweeter far
Than the crooning of old Kevin's pipes beyond
    in Coolnagar.

[31]

I was bound for the milking with a heart fair
  and free—
My grief! my grief! that bitter hour drained
  the life from me.
I thought him human lover, though his lips
  on mine were cold,
And the breath of death blew keen on me within
  his hold.

I know not what way he came, no shadow
  fell behind,
But all the sighing rushes swayed beneath a
  faery wind,
The thrush ceased its singing, a mist crept
  about,
We two clung together—with the world shut
  out.

Beyond the ghostly mist I could hear my cattle
  low,
The little cow from Ballina, clean as driven
  snow,
The dun cow from Kerry, the roan from
  Inisheer,
Oh, pitiful their calling—and his whispers in
  my ear!

His eyes were a fire; his words were a snare;
I cried my mother's name, but no help was
    there;
I made the blessed Sign; then he gave a dreary
    moan,
A wisp of cloud went floating by, and I stood
    alone.

Running ever through my head, is an old-time
    rune—
"Who meets the Love-Talker must weave
    her shroud soon."
My mother's face is furrowed with the salt
    tears that fall,
But the kind eyes of my father are the saddest
    sight of all.

I have spun the fleecy lint, and now my wheel
    is still,
The linen length is woven for my shroud fine
    and chill.
I shall stretch me on the bed where a happy
    maid I lay—
*Pray for the soul of Mairé Og at dawning of the
    day!*

C

Nora Hopper Chesson
(1871–1906)

THE KING OF IRELAND'S SON

Now all away to Tir na n'Og are many roads
    that run,
But he has ta'en the longest lane, the King of
    Ireland's son.

Where Aongus goes there's many a rose burns
    red mid shadows dun;
No rose there is will draw his kiss, the King
    of Ireland's son.

And yonder, where the sun is high, Love laughs
    amid the hay,
But smile and sigh have passed him by, and
    never make delay.

And here (and O! the sun is low!) they're
    glad for harvest won,
But naught he cares for wheat or tares, the King
    of Ireland's son!

And you have flung love's apple by, and I'm
    to pluck it yet;
But what are fruits of gramarye with Druid
    dews beset?

Oh, what are magic fruits to him who meets
    the Lianan-sidhe
Or hears athwart the distance dim Fionn's horn
    blow drowsily !

He follows on for ever when all your chase
    is done,
He follows after shadows, the King of Ireland's
    son.

SOONTREE
A Lullaby

My joy and my grief, go sleep and gather
Dreams from the tree where the dreams hang
    low,
Rounder than apples, and sweeter than honey,
All to delight you, *ma creevin cno !*

My joy, fill your dear hands full of roses,
And gather lilies that stand a-row :
Pull rush and reed with the Shee's fair children,
But eat not, drink not, *ma creevin cno !*

You may not taste of the cups of honey,
You may not taste of the wine blood-red.
Of the mead and the wine he drank, your father,
And the next night's rain wept your father, dead.

Reach up to the star that hangs the lowest,
Tread down the drift of the apple-blow,
Ride your ragweed horse to the Isle of Nobles;
But the Shee's wine drink not, *ma creevin cno!*
    Shoheen, shoheen, shoheen, sho!

THE FAIRY FIDDLER

'Tis I go fiddling, fiddling,
  · By weedy ways forlorn:
I make the blackbird's music
  Ere in his breast 'tis born:
The sleeping larks I waken
  Twixt the midnight and the morn.

No man alive has seen me,
  But women hear me play
Sometimes at door or window
  Fiddling the souls away,—
The child's soul and the colleen's
  Out of the covering clay.

None of my fairy kinsmen
  Make music with me now:
Alone the raths I wander
  Or ride the whitethorn bough,
But the wild swans they know me,
  And the horse that draws the plough.

Nora Hopper Chesson

A CONNAUGHT LAMENT

I WILL arise and go hence to the west,
And dig me a grave where the hill-winds call;
But O were I dead, were I dust, the fall
Of my own love's footstep would break my
    rest!

My heart in my bosom is black as a sloe!
I heed not cuckoo, nor wren, nor swallow:
Like a flying leaf in the sky's blue hollow
The heart in my breast is, that beats so low.

Because of the words your lips have spoken
(O dear black head that I must not follow),
My heart is a grave that is stripped and hollow,
As ice on the water my heart is broken.

O lips forgetful and kindness fickle,
The swallow goes south with you: I go west,
Where fields are empty and scythes at rest.
I am the poppy and you the sickle;
My heart is broken within my breast.

THE CUCKOO SINGS IN THE HEART OF WINTER.

THE cuckoo sings in the heart of winter,
  And all for Mauryeen he tunes his song;
How Mauryeen's hair is the honey's colour.
  (He sings of her all the winter long!)

Her long loose hair's of the honey's colour,
  The wild sweet honey that wild bees make;
The sun herself is ashamed before her,
  The moon is pale for her gold cool's sake.

She bound her hair of the honey's colour
  With flowers of yarrow and quicken green,
And now one binds it with leaves of willow,
  And cypress lies where my head has been.

Now robins sing beside Pastheen's doorway,
  And wrens for bounty that Grania gave:
The cuckoo sings in the heart of winter;
  He sings all day beside Mauryeen's grave.

Wilfred Rowland Childe
(1890–   )

THE SPLENDID ROAD

WISER was he than the King Solomon,
Blue were his eyes and deeper than deep wells,
He walked upon the open road, alone,
And from the dim south came a sound of bells.
A pilgrim's staff within his hand there was,
With fair, fine scarlet was he clad upon,
Walking, he dreamed of builded chrysopras,
And of that place, where on a regent throne
The white rose of celestial virgins is,
Mary, God's Mother, and his mother too,
Midmost of those translunar palaces.
Wiser was he than the King Solomon,
That walked to Walsingham under the blue,
Dreaming of Syon, on the road alone.

PRAYER OF THE PILGRIM TO BEAUTY

I HAVE loved many; there remains but one,
White as the snow beneath the virgin sun,
Within whose eyes a taper burns of bright
      Lovely shrine-guarding light.

O thou who once beneath a night of stars
Didst break for me the dull world's prison bars,
And on the blue top of a hill didst give
    Thy soul, by which I live—

Hereby I do renounce, abjure, remove,
All other soiled idolatries of love,
And thee replace, where thou must rule alone,
    Upon my spirit's throne! . . .

AGE GOTHIQUE DORÉ

(For Daniel Gill)

KING RICHARD in his garden walks royal,
His mantle green being wrought with scarlet
    flowers,
His hand holding a coloured book of hours,
His coat all gold, gilden his feet withal.
King Richard walks in his garden by Thames-
    side,
Hearing the bells of high Westminster ring,
And the sound of the chant of the monks
    echoing,
Singing each in his stall to God Crucified.
Golden the sun descends beyond Thames-water,
Golden flash out London steeples and spires,
The vanes burn and turn in the day's last fires.

About the King the flowers of the garden fade,
And in star-light he walks on, yet lonelier,
His heart being filled with the peace of the
    Mother Maid.

THE GOTHIC ROSE

AMID the blue smoke of gem-glassed chapels
You shall find Me, the white five-wounded
    Flower,
The Rose of Sarras. Yea, the moths have eaten
And fretted the gold cloths of the Duke of York,
And lost is the scarlet cloak of the Cardinal
    Beaufort ;
Tapers are quenched and rods of silver broken,
Where once King Richard dined beneath the
    leopards :
But think you that any beautifulness is wasted,
With which Mine angels have blessed the blue-
    eyed English,
Twining into stone an obscure dream of Heaven,
A crown of flinty spines about the Rose,
A slim flame blessing the Coronal of Thorns ?
And York is for ever the White Rose of Mary,
And Lancaster is dipt in the Precious Blood,

Though the high shrine that was built by the
    king of the Romans
Be down at Hayles, and the abbey of Saint Mary
Be shattered now in three-towered Eboracum.

MOYEN AGE

By the door in the wall of Saint Symeon's
    minster,
    That looketh toward the eastern hill,
There groweth an elder; one morning in May-
    time
    A Bird sang there with a golden bill,

While the white-robed monks were chanting
    at Matins,
    And the wind blew sweet over meadows of
    flowers,
And high in the wind o'er Saint Symeon's
    minster
    The daws were wheeling around the towers.

Young Jankyn, son of a miller in Flock Street,
    Passed by the door with his flute in his hand,
And he heard the song of the Bird in the elder,
    And he wept for joy at the blossomy land.

This is the song of the Bird in the elder,
  As Jankyn afterward wrote it down—
"The dreams that visit the hearts of children
  Shall lead in the end to the Perfect Crown."

Jankyn is carven in alabaster,
  On his tomb three laurelled Angels nod,
And the songs which he made endure for ever:
  For the Bird was a Spirit sent from God.

PRE-RAPHAELITE SPRING

When the black rains were over,
  There came a brightening at even;
A cloud like a dove's pinion
  Brooded across the West;
The garden pools shone glistening,
  A starling preened his feathers,
The sky was all one blessing,
  Gray dove-wing, gray dove-breast.

This was the hour of sunset,
  When the tall trees dripped rain-tears;
The sodden earth exhaling
  In gentle mist lay still;

Deep down in her drenchen bosom
  The dreaming seeds were quickened,
Crocus and lily and lupin,
  Daisy and daffodil.

O dove-wings in the sunset
  On an evening of January,
When all day long had thundered
  The drumming hooves of the rain,
And looking out from my window
  I saw that Northern garden
Folded beneath those dove-wings,
  Weary after her pain!

A. E. Coppard
(1878–   )

EASTER DAY

CALM and courteous was the day
As I, with pleasure toiling,
Combed at the moss in the lawn beneath my
    cedar ;
A calm and courteous day,
Brooding as silent as a swan,
His feet among the lilies.

But visions oft are fairer than the view.
Immuring Time unseals a moment's dream :
Belauded Venus shines,
Makes mock of pontiffs and connives with
    thieves,
And the eye of faith pursues her :
So I thought of princes' daughters
And dreamed of a harp of gold.

The harp had lost its music,
Its strings were torn,
And all its airs were banished
To sigh unborn.

As I was pleasantly toiling
A cloud, a cinder-coloured cloud,
Ophidian, sly, congealed,
Crawled past the hornbeam trees,
Threshing out stones of hail from its bursting
    sack,
Piling frail opulence on lawn, tower, roof and
    tree.
Then I hear the voice of my joy ;
And my little one comes out in rubber shoes,
Trailing her yellow doll called Custard Spoon,
To dance in the showers of hail
Under a red umbrella.

I call to her with love but she does not hear;
Putting the frozen pearls between her lips,
"How cold you are," she sighs,
"I will not stay with you."
And the child goes, and my joy goes,
And fast flies the squall.

Love is an easy gift,
But love is hard to win.
Yet why should this harass me,
Who am but a mote
Brushed from divinity's eye?
Time cannot breed the phœnix,
Nor the sea o'erleap its waves.
But the squall dies, and the sun renews its
     beams
So calm and courteous;
Small clouds are feathers, blown
White ferns in a grove of blue
Over the hornbeam trees.

I comb and comb and comb at the spicy moss,
All day I am pleasantly toiling,
And the red umbrella lies on the lawn unfolded.

A. E. Coppard

CONCLUSION

I COULD recall—yet why recall
Beguiling beauty, ever prone
To scorn the homage it has won?
Time upon all lets the dull latch fall.

I could prolong—yet why prolong
The dream of days that were no dream?
Apples unplucked must fall, I deem,
Or rot no matter where they hung.

Frances Cornford
(1886–   )

A FRAGMENT OF EMPEDOCLES

I HEARD a thrush sing in the flowering may,
  All in the morning cool,
Whilst Joan and Jack ran to the river to play
  And found a silvery salmon in a pool.

Now all these five fair things, I wished them
        joy—
  Kindred and close to me:
"For I have been, ere now, a girl and a boy,
  A bush, a bird, and a dumb fish in the sea."

[47]

Robert Crawford
(1877–1931)

I TOOK MY LOVE

I TOOK my love by a woodside
Which soft grass washes like a tide,
Where drunk bees stagger past the ear,
From Inn to Inn with sudden cheer.

To warm her love I wished her brought
Where the bee sings and Time is nought,
And over Clyde's impassioned skies
The air breaks into butterflies.

I took her where the wanton flowers
Can keep the sunshine after hours,
And daisies' Puritan-caress
Might teach the kiss of holiness;

And stayed while beams drew slant, too soon
That soft glow makes an afternoon;
Then like a wild bird in her side,
Her heart sprang up at eventide.

Henry Cust
(1861–1917)

Not unto us, O Lord,
Not unto us the rapture of the day,
The peace of night, or love's divine surprise,
High heart, high speech, high deeds 'mid
    honouring eyes;
For at Thy word
All these are taken away.

Not unto us, O Lord:
To us Thou givest the scorn, the scourge, the
    scar,
The ache of life, the loneliness of death,
The insufferable sufficiency of breath;
And with Thy sword
Thou piercest very far.

Not unto us, O Lord:
Nay, Lord, but unto her be all things given—
May light and life and earth and sky be blasted—
But let not all that wealth of loss be wasted:
Let Hell afford
The pavement of her Heaven!

COME, MELANCHOLY

COME, Melancholy, come, Delight :
    Let's croak of misery, like a frog.
Let us pretend the window's shut
    For the cat, and a door for the dog.
Let us pretend that every door's
    Made fast, to all except the Bee—
Who finds a key-hole every time,
    And passes in without a key.
Let us pretend that Life's a babe
    All wrapt in clay, with pins of ice,
Without a nurse to tuck it in,
    Or soothe it with a softer voice.
And when we have imagined these,
    Refusing peace, and scorning mirth—
We'll light our pipes and blow a smoke
    That casts a halo on our birth !

IN WINTER

THE World dictates my life from day to day,
    It holds my purse, and cuts my pleasures
        down,
If I would ride, it tells me I must walk,
    It counts my concerts, when I live in Town.

Yet when I see yon lovely hill this morning,
　All white and sepia with its trees and snow—
Who'll think I'd be a wiser, better man
　To sit in cushions at a gilded show?
So let the World dictate my daily life,
　Let beauty last, till Summer brings me more—
Where lovers, paired together, laugh and play,
　As they go wobbling sideways past my door.

AGE AND YOUTH

THE music's dull—I trust my Ears;
　The day is cold—I blame no Blood;
The air has mist—I trust my Eyes;
　My bread is stale—my Teeth hold good;
My bed is hard—I blame no Bones;
My drink is sour—I trust my Tongue.
　Ears, Blood and Eyes; Teeth, Tongue and
　　　Bones—
　　　　Tell me what's wrong,
　　　　And speak the truth.
" It's strange, Old Man, but no complaint
　　Has come from Youth."

William MacNeile Dixon
(1866–1946)

MONSERRATE ADIEU!

So FADES the vision and so flit the shades,
  To the dim underworld of memory,—
The palms, the woody terraces, the glades,
  The shining plain, Collares and the sea.

Below the margin of the world extreme
  The starry hours dip from the wheeling pole,
And Bella Vista, Penha Verde seem
  But fairy pictures of the dreaming soul.

Wide are the seas, and with new friends you
      may
  To many shores and many havens come,
But we alone can to each other say,
  "Once we took ship and found Elysium."

EXSEQUIÆ

WHEN the house is haunted by death,
  The spectre unseen and unheard,
And the living are scant of their breath,
  Though the sleeper hears never a word:

When the grave-sward is trampled to clay,
  And the drip of the world-blotting rain
From skies of a passionless grey
  Beats true to the pulses of pain;

O Father and Maker and God!
  How falters the heart of thy child,
How breathless and cold is the sod,
  How lonely the infinite wild!

E. R. Dodds
(1893–   )

WHEN THE ECSTATIC BODY GRIPS

WHEN the ecstatic body grips
  Its heaven, with little sobbing cries,
And lips are crushed on hot blind lips,
  I read strange pity in your eyes.

For that in you which is not mine,
  And that in you which I love best,
And that, which my day-thoughts divine
  Masterless still, still unpossessed,

E. R. Dodds

Sits in the blue eyes' frightened stare,
  A naked lonely-dwelling thing,
A frail thing from its body-lair
  Drawn at my body's summoning;

Whispering low, " O unknown man,
  Whose hunger on my hunger wrought,
Body shall give what body can,
  Shall give you all—save what you sought."

Whispering, " O secret one, forgive,
  Forgive and be content though still
Beyond the blood's surrender live
  The darkness of the separate will.

" Enough if in the veins we know
  Body's delirium, body's peace—
Ask not that ghost to ghost shall go,
  Essence in essence merge and cease."

But swiftly, as in sudden sleep,
  That You in you is veiled or dead;
And the world's shrunken to a heap
  Of hot flesh huddled on a bed.

Lord Alfred Douglas
(1870–1945)

THE GREEN RIVER

I KNOW a green grass path that leaves the field,
And, like a running river, winds along
Into a leafy wood, where is no throng
Of birds at noon-day; and no soft throats yield
Their music to the moon. The place is sealed,
An unclaimed sovereignty of voiceless song,
And all the unravished silences belong
To some sweet singer lost, or unrevealed.

So is my soul become a silent place.
Oh may I wake from this uneasy night
To find a voice of music manifold.
Let it be shape of sorrow with wan face,
Or love that swoons on sleep, or else delight
That is as wide-eyed as a marigold.

PERKIN WARBECK

I

AT Turney in Flanders I was born
 Fore-doomed to splendour and sorrow,
For I was a king when they cut the corn,
 And they strangle me to-morrow.

II

Oh! why was I made so red and white,
 So fair and straight and tall?
And why were my eyes so blue and bright,
 And my hands so white and small?

III

And why was my hair like the yellow silk,
 And curled like the hair of a king?
And my body like the soft new milk
 That the maids bring from milking?

IV

I was nothing but a weaver's son,
 I was born in a weaver's bed;
My brothers toiled and my sisters spun,
 And my mother wove for our bread.

V

I was the latest child she had,
 And my mother loved me the best.
She would laugh for joy and anon be sad
 That I was not as the rest.

VI

For my brothers and sisters were black as the
    gate
  Whereby I shall pass to-morrow,
But I was white and delicate,
  And born to splendour and sorrow.

VII

And my father the weaver died full soon,
  But my mother lived for me ;
And I had silk doublets and satin shoon
  And was nurtured tenderly.

VIII

And the good priests had much joy of me,
  For I had wisdom and wit ;
And there was no tongue or subtlety
  But I could master it.

IX

And when I was fourteen summers old
  There came an English knight,
With purple cloak and spurs of gold,
  And sword of chrysolite.

X

He rode through the town both sad and slow,
  And his hands lay in his lap ;
He wore a scarf as white as the snow,
  And a snow-white rose in his cap.

XI

And he passed me by in the market-place,
  And he reined his horse and stared,
And I looked him fair and full in the face,
  And he stayed with his head all bared.

XII

And he leaped down quick and bowed his knee,
  And took hold on my hand,
And he said, " Is it ghost or wraith that I see,
  Or the White Rose of England ? "

XIII

And I answered him in the Flemish tongue,
  " My name is Peter Warbeckke,
From Katherine de Faro I am sprung,
  And my father was John Osbeckke.

XIV

" My father toiled and weaved with his hand
    And bore neither sword nor shield,
And the White Rose of fair England
    Turned red on Bosworth field."

XV

And he answered, "What matter for anything?
    For God hath given to thee
The voice of the king and the face of the king,
    And the king thou shalt surely be."

XVI

And he wrought on me till the vesper bell,
    And I rode forth out of the town:
And I might not bid my mother farewell,
    Lest her love should seem more than a crown.

XVII

And the sun went down, and the night waxed
      black,
    And the wind sang wearily;
And I thought on my mother, and would have
      gone back,
    But he would not suffer me.

XVIII

And we rode, and we rode—was it nine days
    or three ?—
  Till we heard the bells that ring
For " my cousin Margaret of Burgundy,"
  And I was indeed a king.

XIX

For I had a hundred fighting men
  To come at my beck and call,
And I had silk and fine linen
  To line my bed withal.

XX

They dressed me all in silken dresses,
  And little I wot did they reck
Of the precious scents for my golden tresses,
  And the golden chains for my neck.

XXI

And all the path for " the rose " to walk
  Was strewn with flowers and posies,
I was the milk-white rose of York,
  The rose of all the roses.

XXII

And the Lady Margaret taught me well,
    Till I spake without lisping
Of Warwick and Clarence and Isabel,
    And " my father " Edward the King.

XXIII

And I sailed to Ireland and to France,
    And I sailed to fair Scotland,
And had much honour and pleasaunce,
    And Katherine Gordon's hand.

XXIV

And after that what brooks it to say
    Whither I went or why ?
I was as loath to leave my play
    And fight, as now to die.

XXV

For I was not made for wars and strife
    And blood and slaughtering,
I was but a boy that loved his life,
    And I had not the heart of a king.

XXVI

Oh ! why hath God dealt so hardly with me,
   That such a thing should be done,
That a boy should be born with a king's body
   And the heart of a weaver's son ?

XXVII

I was well pleased to be at the court,
   Lord of the thing that seems ;
It was merry to be a prince for sport,
   A king in a kingdom of dreams.

XXVIII

But ever they said I must strive and fight
   To wrest away the crown,
So I came to England in the night
   And I warred on Exeter town.

XXIX

And the King came up with a mighty host
   And what could I do but fly ?
I had three thousand men at the most,
   And I was most loath to die.

XXX

And they took me and brought me to London
    town,
  And I stood where all men might see ;
I, that had well-nigh worn a crown,
  In a shameful pillory !

XXXI

And I cried these words in the English tongue,
  " I am Peter Warbeckke,
From Katherine de Faro I am sprung
  And my father was John Osbeckke.

XXXII

" My father toiled and weaved with his hand,
  And bore neither sword nor shield ;
And the White Rose of fair England
  Turned red on Bosworth field."

XXXIII

And they gave me my life, but they held me fast
  Within this weary place ;
But I wrought on my guards ere a month was
    past,
  With my wit and my comely face.

XXXIV

And they were ready to set me free,
  But when it was almost done,
And I thought I should gain the narrow sea
  And look on the face of the sun,

XXXV

The lord of the tower had word of it,
  And, alas! for my poor hope,
For this is the end of my face and my wit
  That to-morrow I die by the rope.

XXXVI

And the time draws nigh and the darkness
    closes,
  And the night is almost done.
What had I to do with their roses,
  I, the poor weaver's son?

XXXVII

They promised me a bed so rich,
  And a queen to be my bride,
And I have gotten a narrow ditch
  And a stake to pierce my side.

[64]

XXXVIII

They promised me a kingly part
  And a crown my head to deck,
And I have gotten the hangman's cart
  And a hempen cord for my neck.

XXXIX

Oh! I would that I had never been born,
  To splendour and shame and sorrow,
For it's ill riding to grim Tiborne,
  Where I must ride to-morrow.

XL

I shall dress me all in silk and scarlet,
  And the hangman shall have my ring,
For though I be hanged like a low-born varlet
  They shall know I was once a king.

XLI

And may I not fall faint or sick
  Till I reach at last to the goal,
And I pray that the rope may choke me quick
  And Christ receive my soul.

Lord Alfred Douglas

OXFORD REVISITED

(1932)

ALAS! What make you here, poor ghost that
    goes
Where your swift feet of youth so lightly went?
Time has borne down that gracious argument
Which was your advocate where Isis flows
Through Christchurch meadows. Sublimate
    your woes
Among these happy children whose consent
Holds out kind hands; accept the treasure lent,
Unconquered sweetness, death-defying rose.

Would yet this sweetness find an echoed home
Where the dream-builded city's semblance lies
Beyond the stars, could but its silver bell
Out-chime the iron knell of mis-called doom,
How would not Death come kindly with mild
    eyes,
Shining like invocated Uriel?

Ernest Dowson
(1867–1900)

THE PASSING OF TENNYSON

As his own Arthur fared across the mere,
    With the grave Queen, past knowledge of
      the throng,
Serene and calm, rebuking grief and tear,
    Departs this prince of song.

Whom the gods love, Death does not cleave
      nor smite,
  But like an angel, with soft trailing wing,
He gathers them upon the hush of night,
    With voice and beckoning.

The moonlight falling on that august head,
    Smoothed out the mark of Time's defiling
      hand,
And hushed the voice of mourning round his
      bed—
    " He goes to his own land."

Beyond the ramparts of the world, where stray
    The laurelled few o'er fields Elysian,
He joins his elders of the lyre and bay,
    Led by the Mantuan.

We mourn him not, but sigh with Bedivere,
  Not perished be the sword he bore so long,
Excalibur, whom none is left to wear—
  His magic brand of song.

FANTASIE TRISTE

To my first love
Loved all above;
In late spring;
Pansies, pansies
Such strong fancies
Was all I had to bring.

To my last love
Loved all above:
At evening
Of autumn
One chrysanthemum
Is all I have to bring.

O first, be last
In a dim past!
With the dead flowers
And the strayed hours
There are no flowers left to bring
There are no songs left to sing
Let be at last.

John Drinkwater
(1882–1937)

ROTATION

EVEN the owls are lyrical
  When the moon's right,
And we have no patience with the stars
  On a dusty night.

Love is dull with the mood wrong,
  And age may outsing youth,
For there is no measuring a song,
  Nor counting upon truth.

All's well, and then a flood of loss
  Surges upon delight,
While the rose buds upon the cross,
  And the blind have sight.

Morning wisdom vanishes,
  And dusk brings dread
That stalwart sleep banishes
  Ere primes are said.

He who is sure, has all to learn;
  Who fears, but fears in vain?
For never a day does the year turn,
  But it shall turn again.

SUMMER'S END

Go, green-man Summer, get you hence,
　Your mistress Autumn bids you go;
The larches of your innocence
　Burn out; your virgins are the sloe.

Your pools grow dark; your groves are rust;
　Your withered stalks are rank with dew;
Your poppies are a little dust;
　Your martins have forsaken you.

Beautiful garlands of decay
　Seal up your song and quench your light;
No more at eve the ghost of day
　Lingers with you to keep the night.

The canker that your roses feared,
　Itself is clay; and clay the rose;
Your woodbine now is old-man's-beard—
　You have no further lease of those.

Lest memory were too great a cost,
　Our joy of you with you shall set,
And we will grieve our Summer lost,
　And, even as we grieve, forget.

RENEWAL

THE shadows of the woods are glowing now
Again, beech-leaf and moss, with violets ;
Under the thorn the primroses are lying
Again in the bright bliss of the gendering sun ;
The year forgets
The unbudded bough,
Forgets the long prophetic labour done ;
The sapling rod
In peel and pith quickens, a passion crying,
No more in winter continence to dissemble ;
And love, half-satyr and half-god,
Goes crashing through the brake, his young
 limbs flashing,
And all the Dryads tremble.

THE PASSING OF A STOIC

Now stiff who once was willow,
Now bent who once was tall,
He walks along the garden
At noon and afternoon,
And while the buds are yellow
His life is at the fall,
Yet will he ask no pardon
Who never asked a boon.

[71]

With death he will not quarrel
Nor bid the gods be kind,
The shadow of disaster
Has been his place of school,
And now he makes no moral
Of echoes in his mind
That tell of life the master
With whips for man the fool.

With eyes upon the gravel
He does not heed the year,
Among the lives that waken
He moves but does not live,
A bitter way to travel
He travels without fear,
But with no blessing taken
Goes on with none to give.

AUDIT

Was it not well on clear December nights
  Upon that Kentish road to reach the gate,
See the blue shutters and the golden lights,
  Knowing that eager Love was there to wait
His traveller loves, his ministers, his own,
  His truants still returning late or soon
To share his kindling logs with him alone,
  Warming their lives under a frosty moon?

Was it not well? And of that providence
   Behold, our promised land.   The year is now
All seasons glad with industry, and thence
   What fuller fruit shall come upon the bough?
The year is ours, its pastures, and for us
   To prosper Time that makes us prosperous.

SONNET
(To Tanya—Fairford, April, 1926)

WE have laid up simples against forgetfulness,
   For we the nesting missel-thrush have seen
Brooding above the weaving water-cress;
   We have gone by water-meadows fresh and
      green
Studded with kingcups and with cuckoo-
      flowers,
   By hedges newly fledged with blackthorn
      foam,
And rested, weary with the happy hours,
   At twilight by the kindled hearth of home.

This was our spring, our lucky Eastertide,
   By willowed brooks, and from a western shire
We shared a Monday of the undaunted pride
   Of him who sang the old, the heart's desire;
England we were; and yet of England own
   The budding bough, the song, the builded
      stone.

John Eglinton
(1868–   )

" Who are the winds ?   Who are the winds ? "
   The storm was blowing wild—
" Who are the winds ?   Who are the winds ? "
   So question'd me the wild-eyed child.

" They are the souls, O child," I said,
   " Of men who long since ceased to hope ;
And lastly, wishing to be dead,
   They lay down on the mountain-slope,
   And sighed their wills away ,
And nature taking them hath made
   Round and about the world to stray.
Yet oft is waked the fitful pain,
   Which causes them to blow,
And still the passion stirs again
   Which vex'd them long ago ;
And then no longer linger they,
But with a wild shriek sweep away,
And the green waves whiten to the moon,
And ships are wreck'd, and shores are strewn."

Havelock Ellis
(1859–1939)

IN THE STRAND

FACES I see, as through the street I go,
Scarred by disease and sin that burn like fire,
.And eyes with cold dead light of base desire,
Thin lips sucked in by self-absorption so
One scarce can tell if they are human or no,
Boys whose young candour dies within this
    mire,
Silly girl-faces that are fair for hire,
And over all a mesh of lies.
                   I know
How taint of blood, gold-worship, passion's
    tide,
Curse of self-seeking, lovelessness of hell,
Do mould men's forms for ever, as a glove
Is moulded by the living hand inside ;
All this, I say, I know, and know as well,
I never knew a heart I might not love.

Michael Field

KATHERINE BRADLEY (1846–1914)

EDITH COOPER (1862–1913)

THE TRAGIC MARY QUEEN OF SCOTS

I COULD wish to be dead!
Too quick with life were the tears I shed,
Too sweet for tears is the life I led;
And ah, too lonesome my marriage bed!
    I could wish to be dead.

I could wish to be dead,
For just a word that rings in my head;
Too dear, too dear are the things he said,
They must never be rememberèd.
    I could wish to be dead.

I could wish to be dead.
The wish to be loved is all mis-read,
And to love, one learns when one is wed,
Is to suffer bitter shame; instead
    I could wish to be dead.

BURY HER AT EVEN

BURY her at even
That the stars may shine
Soon above her,
And the dews of twilight cover:
Bury her at even,
Ye that love her.

Bury her at even,
In the wind's decline;
Night receive her
Where no noise can ever grieve her!
Bury her at even,
And then leave her!

TOO LATE

"O VIRGINS, very lovely in your troop,
    O Virgins very lovely, very white,
How is it that your lilies droop?
    How is it that the lamps you bear are not
        alight?

Why are you bending downward from the hill?
    Bright is it on the hill as for a feast."
Trembling they sped as to fulfil
    Some grievous prophecy; nor heeded me
        the least.

Downward they passed. . . . Oh, they were
    very fair,
  But stricken as is frosted April bloom!
Their eyes I saw. . . . Bright with despair
  Their eyes were very lamps to light them to
    their doom.

Full were their looks of love and sorrowing
  As they passed by me, shaking out a spell
Of sighs, of balms. And is it such a thing
  Can be, that they were hurrying to Hell?

John Freeman
(1880–1929)

THE NIGHTINGALE'S SONG

The blackbird's song is lively joy,
The thrush's note sharp tears;
The nightingale's a bitter ecstasy,
And whoso hears

Forgets not though he never hear
The nightingale again
A whispering edge of shadowy wood
And evening rain,

Or dusty streets where April's known
But in high cloud,
Or water poured from lonely hills
In a noisy flood,

Or a child's eyes wandering in deep
Dream-haunted reverie—
These; and the nightingale is heard
Again in misery.

And the sky's full again with stars
Halted in their great march,
And dark winds fold their wings, and night's
High luminous arch

Echoes again, again, again, again,
Infinitely on and on;
And all the world's a dream until
The dream is gone.

MISADVENTURE

You waited there two hours for me while I
Waited elsewhere two long long hours for you.
And then crawled home alone and miserably,
And met you crawling miserably home too.

How we reproached each other, sneered and
    snarled,
Then slept, and waking, looked back at yesterday,
As one may look at a broad tree, grey and
    gnarled,
And saying, What a wreck! saunter away.
Lord, what a wasted evening, we both said,
And then the sun rose in our eyes again;
We saw no more the gnarled tree, grey and dead,
But were as bright as primroses in a dark lane.
And I know not what brings this back to me,
But I was thinking, supposing you and I
Wait so again—impatiently for me
You in your heaven, I for you—O why,
But what fools to wait and wait and wait,
Missing each other for all eternity:
Don't we know now there's only love and hate
Not distant heaven and hell for you and me!
—And look, the low sun fingering the late
Bronze leaves—and hark, the wind upon the sea!

Alice Furlong
(1871–)

I WILL FORGET

I will forget
The moaning of the sea about Aran;
    Green beaches wet,
    And grey rocks barren—
The sea-moan, against rocks that hinder and let!
(I said, and in my saying, remembered yet.)

    I am the cry of the sea
        Moaning about the rocks of Aran.
Ye are the rocks, cold rocks unmoved by me,
        O dark-eyed people of Aran.

    I will forget
The dark-eyed people of the Isles of the Old
        Sea:
Mairead-bheag, and Donal who talked with the
        Sidh.
The dark-eyed people have their own fret,
        Have their own glee.
        I will forget.
(I say, and in my saying, remember yet.)

John Gawsworth
(1912–   )

FROM THE DEEP
(*For Patricia Wood*)

WHEN women look upon their lovers
   They do not see their loves, but gaze
Out on a landscape where their fancy,
   Like sunshine, plays.

When women speak unto their lovers
   Often they do not choose their words,
But loose, unwitting, on bright pinions,
   Phantasmal birds.

ROMAN HEADSTONE

JULIA, *carissima Julia*,
Strange how you hold a beauty for me now,
As though no sixteen centuries had dimmed your
   charm,
When only crusted stones remain to trace
Your exile life, here where I seek not balm
To heal such wounds of body as once scarred
   your lord,
But silence for my mind and peace for hands
That they may cease their restless artifice
And stretch at ease in tendrils and grass strands!

[82]

Julia, carissima Julia,
Strange that no woman bears the likeness now
That you have set upon my tablet mind,
Not in obliterated text as here
In perpetuum ave carved I find,
A valediction lichenised and broken!
Beyond what ultimate are you? I ponder.
In perpetuum ave atque vale.

Julia, where do you wander?

REGRET

WE will return together and go down
   The strawberry lane that curves to Llanthony,
And trudge across the acres brown
   Of Llanvihangel's lea;

There stare again in citizen amaze
   At speckled fishes in the deepest pool,
And gather nuts through sunniest of days,
   Autumnal cool.

We will return together and go down . . .
   No, not the strawberry lane; for youth has
     fled.
We can never return now, never return:
   The past lies dead.

John Gawsworth

LAST SANCTUARY OF PEACE

LAST sanctuary of peace and quietness,
Hamlet of alder grove and rambling brook,
Outlive this fret, this turmoil, Time's distress;
Take arms against To-day, protect each nook,
Each byre, each cot, each vestige of decay;
Let not To-morrow rob them of their place!
Of our antiquity, they yet must stay
Remnant and record of our ancient race.

Shattered of castle, but of stream serene,
Cultured of orchard, wild of wood and fen,
How may you don new dress, or change a scene
Hallowed by history and the love of men?
Take arms against To-day, stem back the tide!
Where peace has rested, there let peace abide.

Monk Gibbon
(1896–   )

IN EXILE

WHO would have thought a little field,
A patch of green where skies are wide,
The steep lane up a valley, and
Smoke curling upwards from beside
Five lonely trees in that steep part,
Could stir such sadness in the heart?

Monk Gibbon

Who would have thought a little field,
A far-off road, a far-off lane,
A far-off cottage could in time
Wake far-off thoughts with so much pain,
Wake far-off thoughts so hard to stem
A man might fear to think of them?

Stella Gibbons
(1902–   )

WAR SONG OF THE ANGELS

Blow the slow horns through the courts of
      Heaven,
So the sound wanders among the clouds
Whose giant breasts slowly turn to the moon,
Or scud in wild silence past the seven
Fixèd stars that their own light shrouds!

Blow the clear horns while our ranks stream
      slowly
Falling with furled wings through the hush,
With faces colder than moonlight shining
Through the dim clouds, and now the holy
Banners strain in the comets' rush!

Blow the slow horns so the moon's mountains
That never echoed, shall echo loud,
And her still lakes reflect our banners,
And the wind of our passing send up fountains
Of silver dust to the silver cloud.

Blow, trumpeters! Our wings have drawn a
    girdle
Round the uneasy world: not to the skies
And the familiar planets Earth looks up,
But to myriad wings and our calm moonlit
    eyes.
Blow, trumpets! Banners, wave, and slow
    horns sound
Now Heaven's shadow lights the common
    ground.

Wilfrid Gibson
(1878–   )

FLANNAN ISLE

" Though three men dwell on Flannan Isle
To keep the lamp alight,
As we steered under the lee, we caught
No glimmer through the night."

A passing ship at dawn had brought
The news; and quickly we set sail,
To find out what strange thing might ail
The keepers of the deep-sea light.

The Winter day broke blue and bright,
With glancing sun and glancing spray,
While o'er the swell our boat made way,
As gallant as a gull in flight.

But as we neared the lonely Isle,
And looked up at the naked height,
And saw the lighthouse towering white,
With blinded lantern that all night
Had never shot a spark
Of comfort through the dark,
So ghostly in the cold sunlight
It seemed, that we were struck the while
With wonder all too dread for words.

And as into the tiny creek
We stole beneath the hanging crag,
We saw three queer, black, ugly birds—
Too big by far, in my belief,
For cormorant or shag—
Like seamen sitting bolt-upright
Upon a half-tide reef:

But, as we neared, they plunged from sight,
Without a sound or spurt of white.

And still too mazed to speak,
We landed; and made fast the boat;
And climbed the track in single file,
Each wishing he were safe afloat,
On any sea, however far,
So it be far from Flannan Isle:
And still we seemed to climb and climb,
As though we'd lost all count of time,
And so must climb for evermore:
Yet, all too soon, we reached the door—
The black, sun-blistered lighthouse door,
That gaped for us ajar.

As, on the threshold, for a spell,
We paused, we seemed to breathe the smell
Of limewash and of tar,
Familiar as our daily breath,
As though 'twere some strange scent of death:
And so, yet wondering, side by side,
We stood a moment, still tongue-tied:
And each with black foreboding eyed
The door, ere we should fling it wide,
To leave the sunlight for the gloom:

Till, plucking courage up, at last,
Hard on each other's heels we passed,
Into the living-room.

Yet, as we crowded through the door
We only saw a table, spread
For dinner, meat and cheese and bread;
But, all untouched, and no one there:
As though, when they sat down to eat,
Ere they could even taste,
Alarm had come; and they in haste
Had risen and left the bread and meat:
For at the table-head a chair
Lay tumbled on the floor.

We listened; but we only heard
The feeble cheeping of a bird
That starved upon its perch:
And, listening still, without a word,
We set about our hopeless search.

We hunted high, we hunted low;
And soon ransacked the empty house;
Then o'er the Island, to and fro,
We ranged, to listen and to look
In every cranny, cleft or nook

That might have hid a bird or mouse :
But, though we searched from shore to shore,
We found no sign in any place :
And soon again stood face to face
Before the gaping door :
And stole into the room once more
As frightened children steal.

Ay : though we hunted high and low,
And hunted everywhere,
Of the three men's fate we found no trace
Of any kind in any place,
But a door ajar, and an untouched meal,
And an overtoppled chair.

And as we listened in the gloom
Of that forsaken living-room—
A chill clutch on our breath—
We thought how ill-chance came to all
Who kept the Flannan Light :
And how the rock had been the death
Of many a likely lad :
How six had come to a sudden end,
And three had gone stark mad :
And one whom we'd all known as friend
Had leapt from the lantern one still night,

And fallen dead by the lighthouse wall :
And long we thought
On the three we sought,
And on what might yet befall.

Like curs a glance has brought to heel
We listened, flinching there :
And looked and looked on the untouched
    meal
And the overtoppled chair.

We seemed to stand for an endless while,
Though still no word was said,
Three men alive on Flannan Isle,
Who thought on three men dead.

JOHN PATTISON GIBSON

DEAD as the Romans he adored
My father lies—
Yet can I see the light of his keen eyes
Leap, as the glitter of an unsheathed sword,
When, to the clarion of their names, awoke
His proud and eager spirit ; and he spoke
Of Hadrian's Wall, that strides from hill to hill
Along the wave-crest of the Great Whin Sill.

And surely now his spirit stands,
This crystal day,
When the first curlew calls, and bent and brae
Awaken to the Spring, above the lands
Of his heart's love, on Winshiels' windy height,
With eyes that see the rampart, squared and
        white,
New-builded, as when Hadrian first surveyed
Rome's arrogance against the North arrayed!

Oliver St. John Gogarty
(1878–   )

RINGSEND
(After reading Tolstoi)

I WILL live in Ringsend
With a red-headed whore,
And the fan-light gone in
Where it lights the hall-door;
And listen each night
For her querulous shout,
As at last she streels in
And the pubs empty out.
To soothe that wild breast
With my old-fangled songs,
Till she feels it redressed

From inordinate wrongs,
Imagined, outrageous,
Preposterous wrongs,
Till peace at last comes,
Shall be all I will do,
Where the little lamp blooms
Like a rose in the stew;
And up the back-garden
The sound comes to me
Of the lapsing, unsoilable,
Whispering sea.

OUR FRIENDS GO WITH US

OUR friends go with us as we go
    Down the long path where Beauty wends,
Where all we love forgathers, so
    Why should we fear to join our friends?

Who would survive them to outlast
    His children; to outwear his fame—
Left when the Triumph has gone past—
    To win from Age, not Time, a name?

Then do not shudder at the knife
    That Death's indifferent hand drives home,
But with the Strivers leave the Strife,
    Nor, after Cæsar, skulk in Rome.

Douglas Goldring
(1887–   )

CALLE MEMO O LOREDAN

WE were staying (that night) in a very old
    palace—
  Very dark, very large, and sheer to the water
    below.
The rooms were silent and strange, and you were
    frightened ;
  The silver lamp gave a feeble, flickering glow.

And the bed had a high dark tester and carved
    black posts.
  And behind our heads was a glimmer of old
    brocade.
Do you remember ? You thought the shadows
    were full of ghosts,
  And the sound of the lapping water made
    you afraid.

Ah, and your face shone pale, in the gleam of
    that quivering flame !
  And your bosom was rich with the round
    pearls row on row ;
And you looked proud and jewelled, and
    passionate without shame—
  Like some Princess who stooped to her lover,
    a long while ago.

[94]

Douglas Goldring

HAMPSTEAD

Oh, were I but a bad brown ass. . . .

Dear Witch, how can I please?
You love delightful trees,
And buttered scones for tea:
But you don't love me.

The littlest flowers that grow
You find and know;
The smallest bee that lives
Comes home to your hives.
There is not an insect thing,
Beetle, or bird on wing,
But, meeting it, you'll say:
"Good day, my dear, good day!"

Oh, were I but a bad brown ass
That rolls on his back and chews the grass
And daily drags the milkman's cart—
Oh, then I'd find a way to your heart.

Oh, were I but a dog or a duck
I'd have better luck. . . .

Eva Gore-Booth
(1870–1925)

MAEVE OF THE BATTLES

I HAVE seen Maeve of the Battles wandering
over the hill,
   And I know that the deed that is in my heart
is her deed,
And my soul is blown about by the wild wind
of her will,
   For always the living must follow whither
the dead would lead—
I have seen Maeve of the Battles wandering
over the hill.

I would dream a dream at twilight of ease and
beauty and peace—
   A dream of light on the mountains, and calm
on the restless sea;
A dream of the gentle days of the world when
battle shall cease
   And the things that are in hatred and wrath
no longer shall be.
I would dream a dream at twilight of ease and
beauty and peace.

The foamless waves are falling soft on the sands
    of Lissadil
  And the world is wrapped in quiet and a
    floating dream of gray;
But the wild winds of the twilight blow straight
    from the haunted hill
  And the stars come out of the darkness and
    shine over Knocknarea—
I have seen Maeve of the Battles wandering
    over the hill.

There is no rest for the soul that has seen the
    wild eyes of Maeve;
  No rest for the heart once caught in the net
    of her yellow hair—
No quiet for the fallen wind, no peace for the
    broken wave;
  Rising and falling, falling and rising with
    soft sounds everywhere,
There is no rest for the soul that has seen the
    wild eyes of Maeve.

I have seen Maeve of the Battles wandering
    over the hill,
  And I know that the deed that is in my heart
    is her deed,
And my soul is blown about by the wild winds
    of her will,

For always the living must follow whither
    the dead would lead—
I have seen Maeve of the Battles wandering
    over the hill.

Sir Edmund Gosse

(1849–1928)

ON A LUTE FOUND IN A SARCOPHAGUS

WHAT curled and scented sun-girls, almond-
    eyed,
With lotus blossoms in their hands and hair,
Have made their swarthy lovers call them fair,
With these spent strings, when brutes were
    deified
And Memnon in the sunrise sprang and cried,
And love-winds smote Bubastis, and the bare
Black breasts of carven Pasht received the
    prayer
Of suppliants bearing gifts from far and wide!

This lute has outsung Egypt; all the lives
Of violent passion, and the vast calm art
That lasts in granite only, all lie dead;
This little bird of song alone survives,
As fresh as when its fluting smote the heart
Last time the brown slave wore it garlanded.

Gerald Gould
(1885–1937)

QUIET

She whom I love will sit apart,
　　And they whom love makes wise
May know the beauty in her heart
　　By the beauty in her eyes.

Thoughts that in quietness confute
　　The noisy world are hers,
Like music in a listening lute
　　Whose strings no finger stirs.

And in her eyes the shadows move,
　　Not glad nor sad, but strange
With those unchanging dreams that prove
　　The littleness of change.

MORTALITY

In the green quiet wood, where I was used,
　　In summer, to a welcome calm and dark,
I found the threat of murder introduced
　　By scars of white paint on the wrinkled bark.

How few old friends were to be spared!   And
    now
I see my friends with new eyes here in town
—Men as trees walking, and on every brow
A pallid scar, and all to be cut down.

THE HAPPY TREE

THERE was a bright and happy tree;
    The wind with music laced its boughs;
Thither across the houseless sea
    Came singing birds to house.

Men grudged the tree its happy eves,
    Its happy dawns of eager sound;
So all that crown and tower of leaves
    They levelled with the ground.

They made an upright of the stem,
    A cross-piece of a bough they made:
No shadow of their deed on them
    The fallen branches laid.

But blithely, since the year was young,
    When they a fitting hill did find,
There on the happy tree they hung
    The Saviour of mankind.

Gerald Gould

THE COMPANION

He found my house upon the hill.
  I made the bed and swept the floor,
And laboured solitary, till
  He entered at the open door.

He sat with me to break my fast:
  He blessed the bread and poured the wine,
And spoke such friendly words, at last
  I knew not were they his or mine;

But only, when he rose and went
  And left the twilight in the door,
I found my hands were more content
  To make a bed and sweep a floor.

Alexander Gray
(1882–   )

NOCTURNE

Night; the unwelcome sound of rain;
  Streets storm-swept, bleak and bare;
And through the blurred and streaming pane
  An unknown city's flare.

Here have I no remembrancer :
  I have no heart to see
These streets which were so dear to her
  And are so strange to me.

John Gray
(1866–1934)

SOUND

FUMES of dead feasts and half-sped dreams
    retold,
Recall all instruments of subtle mould ;
Rude balalaika ; harp, with voice of gold,
  With heavy limbs and harp-strings gilt ;
  The oboe, half-afraid for guilt ;
Pan's clustered phials, stored with all the notes,
The myriad cries of all his woodland throats,
The mellow wondering the night-fowl hoots,
  And creeping morning's rapture trills,
  That fall in bars of lewd quadrilles ;
Bring cruel bells that scream with lips of jade ;
Bring wooden bells that bark and make afraid ;
And dulcimers that tinkle to their grade ;
  Sombamba's monophonous hum ;
  The laughter of the copper drum ;

The tambour, with its laugh less comatose;
Bring, song-birds' tutors, tiny zuffolos;
Hail, weirdness of the comic mask of those
   Whose fingers crawl on hollow flutes;
    Come, courteous viol, that dilutes
A moment's joy into a life of pain,
Crime into song, its poisonous balm, like rain,
Drips from its wailing in the sufferer's brain;
Come, shrieking siren; pitiless gong;
Unnatural woman, lead the song;
Come all fierce instruments, the bugle blare;
Come, whistling of the fretted steeple, where
The wind grows frightened in the iron stair.

SONG OF THE STARS

MANY the children of men;
Swollen women I love.
Bite, white teeth of the frost;
Toil of the husbandmen lost;
Perish the children of men.
Praise of ease and a quiet lot;
Praise of anise and bergamot;
Praise of the note of the dove;
Many the children of men.

Pale let the worn hands wring,
Worn with labour and prayer;
The harvesters' heap is aflare.
I sing the corpse lying naked and robbed
On the plain's torn bosom; I sing
The cell grown cold where the faint heart
    throbbed.
Bursting life and the song of the thrush;
Joy of gathering; apples blush;
Air serene of the standing corn.
Women are swollen; men are born.

Bind me about in death
With a garland of twisted wheat.

The Hon. Julian Grenfell
(1888–1915)

TO A BLACK GREYHOUND

SHINING black in the shining light,
Inky black in the golden sun,
Graceful as the swallow's flight,
Light as swallow, winged one,
Swift as driven hurricane,

The Hon. Julian Grenfell

Double-sinewed stretch and spring,
Muffled thud of flying feet—
See the black dog galloping,
Hear his wild foot-beat.

See him lie when the day is dead,
Black curves curled on the boarded floor.
Sleepy eyes, my sleepy-head—
Eyes that were aflame before.
Gentle now, they burn no more;
Gentle now and softly warm,
With the fire that made them bright,
Hidden—as when after storm
Softly falls the night.

God of speed, who makes the fire—
God of Peace, who lulls the same—
God who gives the fierce desire,
Lust for blood as fierce as flame—
God who stands in Pity's name—
Many may ye be or less,
Ye who rule the earth and sun:
Gods of strength and gentleness,
Ye are ever one.

INTO BATTLE

THE naked earth is warm with spring,
    And with green grass and bursting trees
Leans to the sun's gaze glorying,
    And quivers in the sunny breeze;
And life is colour and warmth and light,
    And a striving evermore for these;
And he is dead who will not fight;
    And who dies fighting has increase.

The fighting man shall from the sun
    Take warmth, and life from the glowing
        earth;
Speed with the light-foot winds to run,
    And with the trees to newer birth;
And find, when fighting shall be done,
    Great rest, and fullness after dearth.

All the bright company of Heaven
    Hold him in their high comradeship,
The Dog-Star, and the Sisters Seven,
    Orion's Belt and sworded hip.

The woodland trees that stand together,
    They stand to him each one a friend;
They gently speak in the windy weather;
    They guide to valley and ridge's end.

The Hon. Julian Grenfell

The kestrel hovering by day,
    And the little owls that call by night,
Bid him be swift and keen as they,
    As keen of ear, as swift of sight.

The blackbird sings to him, " Brother, brother,
    If this be the last song you shall sing,
Sing well, for you may not sing another ;
    Brother, sing."

In dreary, doubtful, waiting hours,
    Before the brazen frenzy starts,
The horses show him nobler powers ;
    O patient eyes, courageous hearts !

And when the burning moment breaks,
    And all things else are out of mind,
And only joy of battle takes
    Him by the throat, and makes him blind,

Through joy and blindness he shall know,
    Not caring much to know, that still
Nor lead nor steel shall reach him, so
    That it be not the Destined Will.

The thundering line of battle stands,
    And in the air death moans and sings ;
But Day shall clasp him with strong hands,
    And Night shall fold him in soft wings.

George Rostrevor Hamilton
(1888–   )

THE UNATTAINABLE
(1917)

BECAUSE you were
Immoderately beautiful, and made
The sun's superb light by comparison a shade;

Because you were
Miraculously beautiful, and left
The miracle-teeming world of miracle bereft;

Because with one dim-comprehended word
You made all solemn, loud, clear harmonies
    unheard—

Therefore must I unprofitably stray,
Wonderless, sightless, deaf, dark in this noon
    of day.

Kenneth Hare
(1888–   )

STAD DAMME
(To J. G.)

Time was when all her ships bore gold,
   And Damme stood, a Queen of old.
When at God's word the tides receded
   She stood unheeded.

Then fell her towers. The peasant now
   Athwart her harbours drives the plough,
And the historic stones seed over
   With grass and clover.

THE PURITAN

The Puritan through Life's sweet garden goes
To pluck the thorn and cast away the rose,
And hopes to please by this peculiar whim,
The God who fashioned it and gave it him.

[109]

F. R. Higgins
(1896–1941)

SONG FOR THE CLATTER-BONES

GOD rest that Jewy woman,
Queen Jezebel, the bitch
Who peeled the clothes from her shoulder-bones
Down to her spent teats
As she stretched out of the window
Among the geraniums, where
She chaffed and laughed like one half daft
Titivating her painted hair—

King Jehu he drove to her,
She tipped him a fancy beck;
But he from his knacky side-car spoke
" Who'll break that dewlapped neck? "
And so she was thrown from the window;
Like Lucifer she fell
Beneath the feet of the horses and they beat
The light out of Jezebel.

That corpse wasn't planted in clover;
Ah, nothing of her was found
Save those grey bones that Hare-foot Mike
Gave me for their lovely sound;
And as once her dancing body
Made star-lit princes sweat

So I'll just clack: though her ghost lacks a
    back
There's music in the old bones yet.

William Noel Hodgson
(1893–1916)

BEFORE ACTION

By all the glories of the day
    And the cool evening's benison,
By that last sunset touch that lay
    Upon the hills when day was done,
By beauty lavishly outpoured
    And blessings carelessly received,
    By all the days that I have lived,
Make me a soldier, Lord.

By all of all man's hopes and fears,
    And all the wonders poets sing,
The laughter of unclouded years,
    And every sad and lovely thing;
By the romantic ages stored
    With high endeavour that was his,
    By all his mad catastrophes,
Make me a man, O Lord.

I, that on my familiar hill
 Saw with uncomprehending eyes
A hundred of Thy sunsets spill
 Their fresh and sanguine sacrifice,
Ere the sun swings his noonday sword
 Must say good-bye to all of this ;—
 By all delights that I shall miss,
Help me to die, O Lord.

Herbert P. Horne
(1865–1916)

EROTOMACHIA

Lo ! how her eyes, lo ! how her hands,
 How every action, which she hath,
Are ever, through the fallen lands
 Whence is the victory of her path,
Swords, whose dominion knows no bounds ;
 But makes us bleed,
 And need
Her lips to mend the wounds.

Ye blessed arrows of that Dear,
 Make speed, with all your sweet alarms ;
Make speed, that Love may quickly bear
 My piercèd body to her arms :

Haste ye, whose battle knows no bounds;
    But makes us bleed,
           And need
Her lips to mend the wounds.

NEC VIOLÆ SEMPER, NEC HIANTIA LILIA FLORENT;
  ET RIGET AMISSA SPINA RELICTA ROSA

WHY are you fair ? Is it because we know,
  Your beauty stays but for another hour ?
Why are you sweet ? Is it because you show,
  Even in the bud, the blasting of the flower ?
    Is it that we,
      Already in the mind,
    Too surely see
      The thoughtless, ruthless, hurry of the
        wind
      Scatter the petals of this perfect rose ?

Why are you sad ? Is it because our kisses,
  That were so sweet in kissing, now are past ?
But are not all things swift to pass as this is,
  Which we desire to last ?
Being too happy, we may not abide
  Within the happiness, that we possess ;
But needs are swept on by the ceaseless tide
  Of Life's unwisdom, and of our distress :

As if, to all this crowd of ecstasies,
    The present close
Were beauty faded, and deceivèd trust;
Locks, that no hand may braid; dull life-
    less eyes,
    Eyes that have wept their lustre into dust.
    Who knows?

ET SUNT COMMERCIA COELI

I DID not raise mine eyes to hers,
    Although I knew she passed me near:
I said, "Her shadow round me stirs;
    It is enough, that she is here,
And that, for once, my way is hers."

I did not look upon her face,
    I knew with whom her heart confers;
For more, that moment had no place:
    I did not raise mine eyes to hers,
I did not look upon her face.

PARADISE WALK

SHE is living in Paradise Walk,
    With the dirt and the noise of the street;
And heaven flies up, if she talk,
    With Paradise down at her feet.

She laughs through a summer of curls;
　　She moves in a garden of grace:
Her glance is a treasure of pearls,
　　How saved from the deeps of her face!

And the magical reach of her thigh
　　Is the measure, with which God began
To build up the peace of the sky,
　　And fashion the pleasures of man.

With Paradise down at her feet,
　　While heaven flies up if she talk;
With the dirt and the noise of the street,
　　She is living in Paradise Walk.

TO THE FLOWERS, TO WEEP

WEEP, roses, weep; and straightway shed
　　Your purest tears.
Weep, honeysuckles, white and red:
　　And with you, all those country dears;

Violets, and every bud of blue,
　　More blue than skies;
Pinks, cowslips, jasmines, lilies too,
　　Pansies and peonies.

For she, that is the Queen of flowers,
    Though called the least,
Lies drooping beneath dreadful Hours,
    Megaera has from Hell released.

Weep, till your lovely heads are bent :
    Weep, you, that fill
The meadow-corners ; and frequent
    All the green margins of the rill.

Flood, flood your cups with crystal tears,
    Until each leaf,
Each flower, through all the upland, wears
    The dole and brilliance of your grief.

So that the Lark, who had from heaven with-
        drawn,
    Re-sing to you
His song, mistaking noon for dawn,
    And those your tears for dew.

A. E. Housman
(1859–1936)

A SHROPSHIRE LAD: XXXI

On Wenlock Edge the wood's in trouble;
  His forest fleece the Wrekin heaves;
The gale, it plies the saplings double,
  And thick on Severn snow the leaves.

'Twould blow like this through holt and hanger
  When Uricon the city stood:
'Tis the old wind in the old anger,
  But then it threshed another wood.

Then, 'twas before my time, the Roman
  At yonder heaving hill would stare:
The blood that warms an English yeoman,
  The thoughts that hurt him, they were there.

There, like the wind through woods in riot,
  Through him the gale of life blew high;
The tree of man was never quiet:
  Then 'twas the Roman, now 'tis I.

The gale, it plies the saplings double,
  It blows so hard, 'twill soon be gone:
To-day the Roman and his trouble
  Are ashes under Uricon.

LAST POEMS: IX

THE chestnut casts his flambeaux, and the
    flowers
  Stream from the hawthorn on the wind
    away,
The doors clap to, the pane is blind with
    showers.
  Pass me the can, lad; there's an end of May.

There's one spoilt spring to scant our mortal lot,
  One season ruined of our little store.
May will be fine next year as like as not:
  Oh ay, but then we shall be twenty-four.

We for a certainty are not the first
  Have sat in taverns while the tempest hurled
Their hopeful plans to emptiness, and cursed
  Whatever brute and blackguard made the
    world.

It is in truth iniquity on high
  To cheat our sentenced souls of aught they
    crave,
And mar the merriment as you and I
  Fare on our long fool's-errand to the grave.

Iniquity it is; but pass the can.
  My lad, no pair of kings our mothers bore;
Our only portion is the estate of man:
  We want the moon, but we shall get no more.

If here to-day the cloud of thunder lours
  To-morrow it will hie on far behests;
The flesh will grieve on other bones than ours
  Soon, and the soul will mourn in other
    breasts.

The troubles of our proud and angry dust
  Are from eternity, and shall not fail.
Bear them we can, and if we can we must.
  Shoulder the sky, my lad, and drink your
    ale.

Douglas Hyde
(1860–   )

MY GRIEF ON THE SEA
(*From the Irish*)

My grief on the sea,
  How the waves of it roll!
For they heave between me
  And the love of my soul!

Douglas Hyde

Abandoned, forsaken,
   To grief and to care,
Will the sea ever waken
   Relief from despair?

My grief, and my trouble!
   Would he and I were
In the province of Leinster,
   Or County of Clare.

Were I and my darling—
   Oh, heart-bitter wound!—
On board of the ship
   For America bound.

On a green bed of rushes
   All last night I lay,
And I flung it abroad
   With the heat of the day.

And my love came behind me—
   He came from the South;
His breast to my bosom,
   His mouth to my mouth.

Douglas Hyde

WERE YOU ON THE MOUNTAIN?
(From the Irish)

O, WERE you on the mountain, or saw you my
    love?
Or saw you my own one, my queen and my
    dove?
Or saw you the maiden with the step firm and
    free?
And say, is she pining in sorrow like me?

I was upon the mountain, and saw there your
    love,
I saw there your own one, your queen and your
    dove;
I saw there the maiden with the step firm and
    free,
And she was *not* pining in sorrow like thee.

I SHALL NOT DIE FOR THEE
(From the Irish)

FOR thee I shall not die,
    Woman high of fame and name;
Foolish men thou mayest slay,
    I and they are not the same.

Why should I expire
 For the fire of any eye,
Slender waist or swan-like limb,
 Is't for them that I should die?

The round breasts, the fresh skin,
 Cheeks crimson, hair so long and rich;
Indeed, indeed, I shall not die,
 Please God, not I, for any such.

The golden hair, the forehead thin,
 The chaste mien, the gracious ease,
The rounded heel, the languid tone,
 Fools alone find death from these.

Thy sharp wit, thy perfect calm,
 Thy thin palm like foam of sea;
Thy white neck, thy blue eye,
 I shall not die for thee.

Woman, graceful as the swan,
 A wise man did nurture me,
Little palm, white neck, bright eye,
 I shall not die for thee.

Selwyn Image
(1849–1930)

A MEDITATION FOR CHRISTMAS

CONSIDER, O my soul, what morn is this!
   Whereon the eternal Lord of all things made,
For us, poor mortals, and our endless bliss,
   Came down from heaven; and, in a manger
     laid,
   The first, rich, offerings of our ransom paid:
Consider, O my soul, what morn is this!

Consider what estate of fearful woe
   Had then been ours, had He refused this
     birth;
From sin to sin tossed vainly to and fro,
   Hell's playthings, o'er a doomed and helpless
     earth!
   Had He from us withheld His priceless
     worth,
Consider man's estate of fearful woe!

Consider to what joys He bids thee rise,
   Who comes, Himself, life's bitter cup to
     drain!
Ah! look on this sweet Child, Whose innocent
     eyes,

Ere all be done, shall close in mortal pain,
  That thou at last Love's Kingdom may'st
    attain :
Consider to what joys He bids thee rise !

Consider all this wonder, O my soul :
  And in thine inmost shrine make music
    sweet !
Yea, let the world, from furthest pole to pole,
  Join in thy praises this dread birth to greet ;
  Kneeling to kiss thy Saviour's infant feet !
Consider all this wonder, O my soul !

HER CONFIRMATION

When my Clorinda walks in white
Unto her Confirmation Rite,
  What sinless dove can show to heaven
A purer sight ?

Beneath a lawn, translucent, crown
Her lovely curls conceal their brown ;
  Her wanton eyes are fastened, even,
Demurely down.

And that delicious mouth of rose
No words, no smile, may discompose :

All of her feels the approaching awe,
And silent grows.

Come, then, Thou noiseless Spirit, and rest
Here, where she waits Thee for her Guest:
   Pass not, but sweetly onward draw,
Till heaven's possessed!

Edgar Jepson
(1863–1938)

THE DESIRE OF WICKED POOR MEN

WE will have violet robes and baths and women,
And drink and talk of beauty and our strife,
On lawns on terraces, under old cedars;
And the far-smiling sea shall lie below us
To rest our eyes on in our silences.
And when we tire of talk there shall be women,
Naked and whitely glimmering in the dusk,
With warm, alluring eyes like misty stars.
And from low boughs loud nightingales shall
    pour
Their poignant and desirous song to thrill
Our tingling nerves to keener ecstasies.
Fainter shall come the sound of distant fiddles,
The echo of the blasted, common world.

Lionel Johnson
(1867–1902)

ASH WEDNESDAY
(*In Memoriam : Ernest Dowson*)

Memento, homo, quia pulvis es !
To-day the cross of ashes marks my brow :
Yesterday, laid to solemn sleep wert thou,
O dear to me of old, and dearer now !
Memento, homo, quia pulvis es !

Memento, homo, quia pulvis es !
And all the subtle beauty of that face,
With all its winning, all its wistful grace,
Fades in the consecrated stilly place :
Memento, homo, quia pulvis es !

Memento, homo, quia pulvis es !
The visible vehement earth remains to me :
The visionary quiet land holds thee :
But what shall separate such friends as we ?
Memento, homo, quia pulvis es !

TO ALFRED FERRAND

Ah, thank whatever Gods you have,
    For granting you a golden art :
For making this side of the grave,
    A stage to play a double part.

Lionel Johnson

Your own and other lives you live :
    I have one only life, my own.
To me my Gods less kindly give
    The music of a monotone.

Yet sometimes, for a little space,
    Pitying my loneliness, they send
To give my days a little grace,
    The goodliest of their gifts, a friend.

Patrick Kavanagh
(1905–   )

PLOUGH-HORSES

THEIR glossy flanks and manes outshone
The flying splinters of the sun.

The tranquil rhythm of that team
Was as slow-flowing meadow stream.

And I saw Phidias' chisel there—
An ocean stallion, mountain mare,

Seeing, with eyes the Spirit unsealed
Plough-horses in a quiet field.

OLD SOLDIER

I RETURN to the land
  Of tillage peace,
Who have wandered and found
  No golden fleece,

But only a rag
  On a lifting thorn—
An ironic flag
  Crow-pecked, forlorn.

Love's frosted buds,
  That could not shake
The nursing gods
  Of green, awake.

Petty squabbling
  My eyes did see,
And Achilles wobbling
  In jeopardy,

And the men of thought
  Being hustled on
Till there was not
  Under the sun

Patrick Kavanagh

An unflustered bird
  Of evening mood
Or a poet's word
  In the interlude.

Over the war-loud
  Fields I went,
Strumming the crowd-
  False instrument,

One with the savage
  And insane . . . .
O War, to ravage
  My virgin Spain!

ETHICAL

You who have not sown
  Will eat the bitter bread
And beg the sweetness of a stone
  Flung at Saint Stephen's head.

You who have not sung
  Will hear the clang of brass
When fairies beat on April's gong
  With stems of greening grass.

And you who have not prayed
   The blackbird's evening prayer
Will kneel all night dismayed
   Upon a frozen stair.

The Hon. Emily Lawless
(1845–1913)

DIRGE OF THE MUNSTER FOREST
(1591)

BRING out the hemlock! Bring the funeral
    yew !
The faithful ivy that doth all enfold ;
Heap high the rocks, the patient brown earth
    strew,
And cover them against the numbing cold.
Marshal my retinue of bird and beast,
Wren, titmouse, robin, birds of every hue ;
Let none keep back, no, not the very least,
Nor fox, nor deer, nor tiny nibbling crew,
Only bid one of all my forest clan
Keep far from us on this our funeral day.
On the grey wolf I lay my sovereign ban,
The great grey wolf who scrapes the earth away ;
Lest, with hooked claw and furious hunger, he
Lay bare my dead for gloating foes to see—
Lay bare my dead, who died, and died for me.

For I must surely die as they have died,
And lo! my doom stands yoked and linked
   with theirs;
The axe is sharpened to cut down my pride:
I pass, I die, and leave no natural heirs.

Soon shall my sylvan coronals be cast;
My hidden sanctuaries, my secret ways,
Naked must stand to the rebellious blast;
No Spring shall quicken what this Autumn
   slays.

Therefore, while still I keep my russet crown,
I summon all my lieges to the feast.
Hither, ye flutterers! black, or pied, or brown;
Hither, ye furred ones! Hither every beast!

Only to one of all my forest clan
I cry, "Avaunt! Our mourning revels flee!"
On the grey wolf I lay my sovereign ban,
The great grey wolf with scraping claws, lest he
Lay bare my dead for gloating foes to see—
Lay bare my dead, who died, and died for me.

AFTER AUGHRIM
(1691)

SHE said, "They gave me of their best,
   They lived, they gave their lives for me;
I tossed them to the howling waste,
   And flung them to the foaming sea."

[131]

She said, "I never gave them aught,
  Not mine the power, if mine the will;
I let them starve, I let them bleed,—
  They bled and starved, and loved me still."

She said, "Ten times they fought for me,
  Ten times they strove with might and main,
Ten times I saw them beaten down,
  Ten times they rose, and fought again."

She said, "I stayed alone at home,
  A dreary woman, grey and cold;
I never asked them how they fared,
  Yet still they loved me as of old."

She said, "I never called them sons,
  I almost ceased to breathe their name,
Then caught it echoing down the wind,
  Blown backwards from the lips of Fame."

She said, "Not mine, not mine that fame;
  Far over sea, far over land,
Cast forth like rubbish from my shores,
  They won it yonder, sword in hand."

She said, "God knows they owe me nought,
  I tossed them to the foaming sea,
I tossed them to the howling waste,
  Yet still their love comes home to me."

The Hon. Emily Lawless

CLARE COAST
(*Circa* 1720)

SEE, cold island, we stand
Here to-night on your shore,
To-night, but never again;
Lingering a moment more.
See, beneath us our boat
Tugs at its tightening chain,
Holds out its sail to the breeze,
Pants to be gone again.
Off then with shouts and mirth,
Off with laughter and jests,
Mirth and song on our lips,
Hearts like lead in our breasts.

Death and the grave behind,
Death and a traitor's bier;
Honour and fame before,
Why do we linger here?
Why do we stand and gaze,
Fools, whom fools despise,
Fools untaught by the years,
Fools renounced by the wise?
Heartsick, a moment more,
Heartsick, sorry, fierce,

Lingering, lingering on,
Dreaming the dreams of yore ;
Dreaming the dreams of our youth,
Dreaming the days when we stood
Joyous, expectant, serene,
Glad, exultant of mood,
Singing with hearts afire,
Singing with joyous strain,
Singing aloud in our pride,
" We shall redeem her again ! "

Ah, not to-night that strain,—
Silent to-night we stand,
A scanty, a toil-worn crew,
Strangers, foes in the land !
Gone the light of our youth,
Gone for ever, and gone
Hope with the beautiful eyes,
Who laughed as she lured us on ;
Lured us to danger and death,
To honour, perchance to fame,—
Empty fame at the best,
Glory half dimmed with shame.
War-battered dogs are we,
Fighters in every clime,
Fillers of trench and of grave,
Mockers, bemocked by time.

War-dogs, hungry and grey,
Gnawing a naked bone,
Fighters in every clime,
Every cause but our own.

See us, cold isle of our love !
Coldest, saddest of isles—
Cold as the hopes of our youth,
Cold as your own wan smiles.
Coldly your streams outpour,
Each apart on the height,
Trickling, indifferent, slow,
Lost in the hush of the night.
Colder, sadder the clouds,
Comfortless bringers of rain ;
Desolate daughters of air,
Sweep o'er your sad grey plain
Hiding the form of your hills,
Hiding your low sand duns ;
But coldest, saddest, oh isle !
Are the homeless hearts of your sons.

Coldest, and saddest there,
In yon sunlit land of the south,
Where we sicken, and sorrow, and pine,
And the jest flies from mouth to mouth,
And the church bells crash overheard,

And the idle hours flit by,
And the beaded wine-cups clink,
And the sun burns fierce in the sky;
And your exiles, the merry of heart,
Laugh and boast with the best,—
Boast, and extol their part,
Boast, till some lifted brow,
Crossed with a line severe,
Seems with displeasure to ask,
" Are these loud braggarts we hear,
Are they the sons of the West,
The wept-for, the theme of songs,
The exiled, the injured, the banned,
The men of a thousand wrongs?"

Fool, did you never hear
Of sunshine which broke through rain?
Sunshine which came with storm?
Laughter that rang of pain?
Boastings begotten of grief,
Vauntings to hide a smart,
Braggings with trembling lip,
Tricks of a broken heart?

Sudden some wayward gleam,
Sudden some passing sound,—

The careless splash of an oar,
The idle bark of a hound,
A shadow crossing the sun,
An unknown step in the hall,
A nothing, a folly, a straw!—
Back it returns—all—all!
Back with the rush of a storm,
Back the old anguish and ill,
The sad, green landscape of home,
The small grey house by the hill,
The wide grey shores of the lake,
The low sky, seeming to weave
Its tender pitiful arms
Round the sick, lone landscape at eve.
Back with its pains and its wrongs,
Back with its toils and its strife,
Back with its struggles and woe,
Back flows the stream of our life,
Darkened with treason and wrong,
Darkened with anguish and ruth,
Bitter, tumultuous, fierce,
Yet glad in the light of our youth.

So, cold island, we stand
Here to-night on your shore,—
To-night, but never again,
Lingering a moment more.

See, beneath us our boat
Tugs at its tightening chain,
Holds out its sail to the breeze,
Pants to be gone again.
Off then with shouts and mirth,
Off with laughter and jests,
Jests and song on our lips,
Hearts like lead in our breasts.

Sylvia Lynd
(1888–   )

COWPER AT OLNEY

In this green valley where the Ouse
   Is looped in many a silver pool,
Seeking God's mercy and his muse
   Went Cowper sorrowful.

Like the pale gleam of wintry sun
   His genius lit the obscure place,
Where, battling with despair, lived one
   Of melancholy's race.

By quiet waters, by green fields,
   In winter sweet as summer hay,
By hedgerows where the chaffinch builds
   He went his brooding way.

And not a berry or a leaf,
  Or stirring bough or fragrant wind,
But, in its moment, soothed the grief
  Of his tormented mind.

And since, like the below
  Of David's shepherd, he was led
By streams and pastures quiet as sleep—
  Was he not comforted ?

S. R. Lysaght
(1870–1941)

A DESERTED HOME

HERE, where the fields lie lonely and untended,
  Once stood the old house grey among the
    trees,
Once to the hills rolled the waves of the corn-
    land—
  Long waves and golden, softer than the sea's.

Long, long ago has the ploughshare rusted,
  Long has the barn stood roofless and forlorn ;
But oh ! far away are some who still remember
  The songs of the young girls binding up the
    corn.

S. R. Lysaght

Here where the windows shone across the
    darkness,
   Here where the stars once watched above
    ⬛⬛⬛⬛⬛⬛⬛⬛⬛⬛ but the sheepfold is empty;
Falls now the rain where the hearth glowed
    of old.

Here where the leagues of melancholy lough-
    sedge
   Moan in the wind round the grey forsaken
    shore,
Once waved the corn in the mid-month of
    autumn,
   Once sped the dance when the corn was on
    the floor.

Hugh MacDiarmid
(1892–   )

A HERD OF DOES
(Gildermorie)

THERE is no doe in all the herd
   Whose heart is not her heart.
O Earth, with all their glimmering eyes
   She sees thee as thou art.

Like them in shapes of fleeting fire
    She mingles with the light
Till whoso saw her sees her not
    And doubts his former sight.

They come and go and none can say
    Who sees them subtly run
If they indeed are forms of life
    Or figments of the sun.

So is she one with Heaven here,
    Confounding mortal eyes,
As do the holy dead who move
    Innumerous in the skies.

But now and then a wandering man
    May glimpse as on he goes
A golden movement of her dreams
    As 'twere a herd of does.

FIRST LOVE

I HAVE been in this garden of unripe fruit
    All the long day,
Where cold and clear from the hard green apples
    The light fell away.

I was wandering here with my own true love,
    But as I bent o'er,
She dwindled back to her childhood again
    And I saw her no more.

A wind sprang up and a hail of buds
    About me rolled,
Then this fog I knew before I was born
    But now—cold, cold!

CATTLE SHOW

I SHALL go among red faces and virile voices,
See stylish sheep, with fine heads and well-
    wooled,
And great bulls mellow to the touch,
Brood mares of marvellous approach, and
    geldings
With sharp and flinty bones and silken hair.

And through th' enclosure draped in red and gold
I shall pass on to spheres more vivid yet
Where countesses' coque feathers gleam and
    glow
And, swathed in silks, the painted ladies are
Whose laughter plays like summer lightning
    there.

Hugh MacDiarmid

THE LITTLE WHITE ROSE
(To John Gawsworth)

THE Rose of all the world is not for me.
I want, for my part,
Only the little white rose of Scotland
That smells sharp and sweet—and breaks the
heart.

SKALD'S DEATH

I HAVE known all the storms that roll.
I have been a singer after the fashion
Of my people—a poet of passion.
   All that is past.
Quiet has come into my soul.
   Life's tempest is done.
   I lie at last
A bird cliff under the midnight sun.

Arthur Machen
(1863-1947)

THE PRAISE OF MYFANWY

O GIFT of the everlasting!
O wonderful and hidden mystery!
Many secrets have been vouchsafed to me.

[143]

I have been long acquainted with the wisdom
    of the trees;
Ash and oak and elm have communicated to
    me from my boyhood,
The birch and the hazel and all the trees of the
    greenwood have not been dumb.
There is a caldron rimmed with pearls of whose
    gifts I am not ignorant.
I will speak little of it; its treasures are known
    to the Bards.
Many went on the search of Caer-Pedryfan,
Seven alone returned with Arthur, but my spirit
    was present.
Seven are the apple-trees in a beautiful orchard.
I have eaten of their fruit, which is not bestowed
    on Saxons.
I am not ignorant of a Head which is glorious
    and venerable.
It made perpetual entertainment for the warriors;
    their joys would have been immortal.
If they had not opened the door of the south,
    they could have feasted for ever,
Listening to the song of the Fairy Birds of
    Rhiannon.
Let not anyone instruct me concerning the
    Glassy Isle,

In the garments of the saints who returned from
    it were the rich odours of Paradise.

All this I knew, and yet my knowledge was
    ignorance,

For one day, as I walked by Caer-rhiu in the
    principal forest of Gwent,

I saw golden Myfanwy, as she bathed in the
    brook Tarógi.

Her hair flowed about her. Arthur's crown had
    dissolved into a shining mist.

I gazed into her blue eyes as it were into twin
    heavens.

All the parts of her body were adornments and
    miracles.

O gift of the everlasting !

O wonderful and hidden mystery !

When I embraced Myfanwy a moment became
    immortality !

THE REMEMBRANCE OF THE BARD

In the darkness of old age let not my memory
    fail,

Let me not forget to celebrate the beloved
    land of Gwent.

If they imprison me in a deep place, in a house
    of pestilence,

Still shall I be free, when I remember the sun-
 shine upon Mynydd Maen.
There have I listened to the singing of the lark,
 my soul has ascended with the song of the
 little bird;
The great white clouds were the ships of my
 spirit, sailing to the haven of the Almighty.
Equally to be held in honour is the site of the
 Great Mountain,
Adorned with the gushing of many waters—
Sweet is the shade of its hazel thickets.
There a treasure is preserved, which I will not
 celebrate,
It is glorious, and deeply concealed.
If Teilo should return, if happiness were restored
 to the Cymri,
Dewi and Dyfrig should serve his Mass; then
 a great marvel would be made visible.
O blessed and miraculous work, then should
 my bliss be as the bliss of angels;
I had rather behold this offering than kiss the
 twin lips of dark Gwenllian.
Dear my land of Gwent, *O quam dilecta taber-
 nacula!*
Thy rivers are like precious golden streams of
 Paradise,

Thy hills are as the Mount Syon—
Better a grave on Twyn Barlwm than a throne
    in the palace of the Saxons at Caer-Ludd.

Hamish Maclaren
(1901–)

ISLAND ROSE
(To J. G.)

SHE has given all her beauty to the water;
    She has told her secrets to the tidal bell;
And her hair is a moon-drawn net, and it has
        caught her,
    And her voice is in the hollow shell.

She will not come back now any more, nor
        waken
    Out of her island dream where no wind blows:
And only in the small house of the shell,
        forsaken,
    Sings the dark one whose face is a rose.

Hamish Maclaren

FURL, seafarers, furl your sails,
No more tempt the clouded seas :
Make not gulls your nightingales
Nor tall masts your cherry-trees.

Trust no song the siren sings,
Softly sounding from afar ;
Sailors, fold your wind-blown wings
And rest where the true voices are.

Ah, be done, you'll find no lands
So honey-sweet, so fair in flocks—
Only the tides, and sinking sands
And sorrow brooding on the rocks.

HIGH NOON

FROM high endeavour
On his bright wings,
The wasp is fallen
To sorry things.

From deep searching
In honey'd cup,
The bee is flown
Elsewhere to sup.

An apple dropped
By a grey trunk—
A wasp wastrel
And a bee drunk!

OCTOBER LOVE LYRIC

THIS night of October,
　When the rain-clouded skies
Are haunted by the memory of starlight,
　I am haunted by your eyes.

And the harvest is over, the harvest,
　Bright barley, sweet hay,
Is gone away love, away love,
　Is gone away.

THE BLUE WIND OF THE YANGTSE VALLEY

THE blue wind from the lake
　Blows, and over me
Sad showers of leaves fall
　To cover me.

Sorrow is in the blue wind;
　There is none to greet now;
And nobody walks by the lotus
　On dainty feet now.

Only the wide-winged cranes
  Fly out of the sunset,
While I in my quilted coat
  Wait winter's onset.

I will set a silver lamp
  In the ly-chee shadows,
And forget that spring ever was
  Sweet in these meadows.

LAKE GARDEN

THEY lie untended :
  Only the dark water shows,
When day's ended
  How they outshine the rose :
The water-lilies
  Break forth in their snows.

They float still and lonely,
  Never a gardener draws near.
The pines, only,
  Stand sentinel about the darkened mere
Where the water-lilies
  Flower year after year.

Edward Powys Mathers
(1892–1939)

ENGLISH GIRL
From the Chinese of J. Wing
(Nineteenth Century)

I THAT lived ever about you
Never touched you, Lilian ;
You came from far away
And devils with twitching faces
Had all their will of you
For gold.
But I saw your little feet in your bedroom,
Your little heathen shoes I kept so bright.
For they regarded not your feet, Lilian,
But I regarded.
Your little heathen stockings were mine to carry
And to set out and to wash.
They regarded not your feet,
But I that lived ever about you
Never touched you, Lilian.
Their faces twitch more this frosty morning ;
They have put you in a heathen box
And hidden your feet and carried you out in
    the frosty morning.
They have passed with you over the foggy brook
And look like big blue men in the mist on the
    other side.

Now only the mist and the water remain.
They never regarded your feet,
But I regarded, Lilian.
Their faces ever twitched,
But for the seven years since I saw you
My face did not change.
They never regarded your warm feet,
But I regarded.

N. K. *McCausland*
(1891–   )

ETAIN

SHE has come from far,
From the Kingdom that must lie
Buried deep beneath the hill,
Shadowed by the evening star;
Bending last year's bracken by,
A bitter hour she shall fulfil;
Cannot the hazel help her
    And the willow,
Or the bank that is her pillow
With its green leaf of goodwill?

She has not far to go
To the Kingdom that must lie
Buried underneath the hill,
Shadowed in the evening glow.
Who can pass those portals by?
She shall dream, and dream her fill;
The hazel bough shall help her
 And the willow,
And the bank that is her pillow
With its green leaf of goodwill.

ALL OUR RIGHTEOUSNESSES ARE AS FILTHY RAGS

She was old, and filled with the thought of the
 grace of God;
 She clothed herself in the words of joy, and
  eternal bliss;
Along the narrow and straitened way, the soul
 of her trod,
 Bearing the hopes of the world beyond, and
  the fears of this.

The Lord was her God. To the poor she had
 given her wealth.
 She had gone with the garment of grace to
  cover their needs;

Stood ever beside them, knowing their weakness
and health.
The Bishop had marvelled and spoken in
praise of her deeds.

She heard them laughing, the young and the
old, as they passed her door;
Their shadows crept over the blind and along
the wall.
She heard the soft slurred tones, the shuffling
feet of the poor.
"I have done what I could," she said, "I
have given them all."

And the poor went out with laughter and
gathered the furze;
They burnt her in effigy, there, on the open
heath.
They had taken her money and food and all
that was hers,
Even the blessing she gave with her dying
breath.

They took what they could and, feeding the
flames, they mocked,
In hatred of her who invaded their homes
at will;

Who entered their lives and their sorrows,
    before she had knocked;
Who spoke the word when their hearts were
    bowed and would fain be still.

How could they understand she was poorer
    than they,
    Than farmer or hind, the man with the fork
      and the cart;
With no splendid possession, no love she might
    give away,
    Only the wish to do right in her narrow heart.

Phyllis Mégroz
(1899–   )

THE SILVER BRIDE

THE Silver Bride, the Silver Bride,
I saw her standing at my side,
The moon fled pallid and dismayed,
The star hosts scattered disarrayed,
The wind stood hesitant and dumb,
And dared not go and dared not come.
No creak of wood, no scuttling mouse
Made friendly clamour in the house.

[155]

All stilled, all tranced, all deathly was,
And through that form as through a glass
Familiar shapes shone strange and clear.
My heart grew cold with coiling fear.
"Why do you seek me, Silver Bride?"
I moaned, and calmly she replied:
"*I am your thought made manifest,*
Possessing me you are possessed,
For you are he whose stinging scorn
Struck every man of woman born,
Broke every link twixt heaven and earth,
These things you said were nothing worth,
And bent your spirit to adore
Your brain and all its garnered store.
I am that brain made manifest,
Possessing me you are possessed.
Link hands, link hands, stoop down and press
My loving lips in long caress.
What! you grow cold, you tremble so,
You would go free? You shall not go."
"O God," I screamed in terror drowned,
"Unlock this house in slumber bound,
One little, common, kindly sound
Grant me to hear for Jesu's grace,
Let me but see one human face
Peer through the window." "Silence!" cried

With splintering mirth the Silver Bride,
"Not Christ Himself, nor any man
Your charmèd circle enter can,
For you have cut the human chain
To kneel in worship to your brain.
I am that brain made manifest,
Possessing me you are possessed.
Lean close, lean closer to my breast."
And I shall never put aside
    The Silver Bride.

IN EXCELSIS

I AM the King of Heaven's daughter,
  The stars uprooted are my crown,
I walk transcendent on the water
  Whose midnight swirl would suck me down.
The hungry winds unleashed as harriers,
  Howl round me clamouring defeat,
The nightmare steeds o'erleap their barriers,
  Beneath the rumour of their feet
The cloud by frantic light is shaken
  And troubled by their fiery breath,
But I, inviolate, untaken,
  Have spanned the curve of life and death,
I am no longer wrung by laughter,
  I am no longer torn by tears,

The ante-natal, the hereafter
    Have no more venom in their spears.
On bloody feet I have arisen
    Between the dark conflicting hours ;
Death, static in the crystal prison,
    In amaranthine blossom cowers,
Shrunk to the spectre of a spectre,
    Whose worlds diminish and grow dim—
Evœ, victrix ! Drain the nectar
    To thy bright God, being born of him.

A false creator leans from heaven,
    And flashes from the ivory gate,
About him wheel the planets seven,
    To him are angels dedicate.
He shakes the skies with hollow thunder,
    He sets awhirl the stellar space,
His lightnings split the cloud asunder,
    And wreathe themselves about his face.
He scatters forth unnumbered seedlings
    That come to short-lived, dwarfish growth,
Coaxed up with smooth, soft words and wheed-
        lings,
    And splintered down with broken troth,
Back to the earth where they were rooted,
    Back to the all-forgetful clay,

Phyllis Mégroz

Unflowered, unfertile and unfruited,
  Pale portents of a finite day
That holds no light but sun, moon, starlight,
  The concrete beauty that must pass,
And knows no glimmer of that far light
  That is the soul's bright burning-glass.
But one not held within the prism,
  The rainbow prism of the air,
Unsealed my spirit with his chrism—
  I travailed darkness and despair.
I saw myself in earth embedded,
  I saw life never satiate,
The miry monster hydra-headed,
  A simulacrum's life create.
I saw Death's sword too worn and blunted
  To cut those febrile fingers through,
And with my naked breast confronted
  The pang immortal that I knew,
So sharp the spirit cannot languish
  Midway between the light and shade,
But is in that vibrating anguish
  Annihilated and remade.

I am compounded of the sexes,
  I am the bridegroom and the bride,
For in the bitter-sweet orexis
  The multiform is unified.

Phyllis Mégroz

I am the King of Heaven's daughter,
  The star beyond the finite stars,
The lily on the tideless water,
  The avatar of avatars.

R. L. Mégroz
(1891–   )

AD PERPETUAM

INCREDIBLE in pride, one year ago,
  You paced the zenith of a wondering mind :
But I, I loved too much.   Your starry glow
  Faith could not reach because his eyes grew
    blind.

Now is that dream at end wherein you moved
  Clad in those regal robes my spirit wove
From shining hours when desperately I loved
  A shade that was the shadow of my love.

How have these wheeling months turned round
    at last
  And summer followed summer, and star star !
You never lived ; but in the heavened past
  My globèd life finds again where bright you
    are.

You never lived? You flame immortally
On my dead world with fire that once was me.

ILLUSION

WHEN Adam spoke for the first time to Eve,
  Breaking the virgin peace of Paradise,
  Was there no veiling of her candid eyes
At the dim thought : *To live is to deceive?*
Or could he not her simple truth believe
  Because already tragically wise
  His heart had heard the serpent's luring lies
Trouble the Eden that they soon must leave?

Airs of strange tenderness steal even now
  From the abandoned Garden, and he hears
Still the same promise while they cool his brow ;
    But Man, in prescient wickedness, knows
      well
  Why he pursues across the flooding years
    Beauty, the bastard child of Heaven and
      Hell.

L

LOVE AND SIN

Two creatures stood by a house, and one went in;
The name of the first was Love, of the other Sin.

Sin seemed a man right fair, with a cheek of joy;
Love was begrimed and patched, like a beggar-
    boy.

Sin brake bolt with a laugh: "Shall we to her
    straight?"
Love knelt down on the step: "Better dream
    and wait!"

Sin sallied forth at dawn with a splendid brow;
"She's awake, brother Love!" he said: "You
    can have her now."

IVY AND HOLLY

ANCIENTLY in this village,
    As true as tale of Troy,
The boys would burn an ivy girl,
    The girls a holly boy.

E. H. W. Meyerstein

Prickly am I as holly,
    Raven as ivy you;
The village burns us on its tongue,
    And all the tale is true.

BLACKAMOOR'S LAMENT

BECAUSE my face is black
    No white maid marries me,
Although my blood I track
    Through loins of Araby.

I know the phœnix well,
    And oft have climbed the palm
Where sprout the twigs that smell
    Over his fiery qualm.

The desert has no pool
    But I have tasted there;
The sultan has no fool
    But I have kissed her hair.

The camel's mountain back
    Bestride I famously;
And yet my face is black;
    No white maid marries me.

Alice Meynell
(1847–1922)

RENOUNCEMENT

I MUST not think of thee ; and, tired yet strong,
I shun the thought that lurks in all delight—
The thought of thee—and in the blue Heaven's
    height,
And in the dearest passage of a song.
Oh, just beyond the fairest thoughts that throng
This breast, the thought of thee waits, hidden
    yet bright ;
But it must never, never come in sight ;
I must stop short of thee the whole day long.
But when sleep comes to close each difficult day,
When night gives pause to the long watch I keep,
And all my bonds I needs must loose apart,
Must doff my will as raiment laid away,—
With the first dream that comes with the first
    sleep
I run, I run, I am gathered to thy heart.

AT NIGHT
(To W. M.)

HOME, home from the horizon far and clear,
    Hither the soft wings sweep ;
Flocks of the memories of the day draw near
    The dovecote doors of sleep.

[164]

Alice Meynell

Oh, which are they that come through sweetest
  light
 Of all these homing birds?
Which with the straightest and the swiftest
  flight?
 Your words to me, your words!

Viola Meynell

(1888–)

JONAH AND THE WHALE

HE sported round the watery world.
 His rich oil was a gloomy waveless lake
Within the waves. Affrighted seamen hurled
 Their weapons in his foaming wake.

One old corroding iron he bore
 Which journeyed through his flesh, but yet
  had not
Found out his life. Another lance he wore
 Outside him pricking in a tender spot.

So distant were his parts that they
 Sent but a dull faint message to his brain.
He knew not his own flesh, as great kings may
 Not know the farther places where they reign.

His play made storm in a calm sea ;
   His very kindness slew what he might touch ;
And wrecks lay scattered on his anger's lee.
   The Moon rocked to and fro his watery couch.

His hunger cleared the sea. And where
   He passed, the ocean's edge lifted its brim.
He skimmed the dim sea-floor to find if there
   Some garden had its harvest ripe for him.

But in his sluggish brain no thought
   Ever arose. His law was instinct blind.
No thought or gleam or vision ever brought
   Light to the dark of his old dreamless mind.

Until one day sudden and strange
   Half-tints of knowledge burst upon his sight.
Glimpses he had of Time, and Space, and Change,
   And something greater than his might ;

And terror's leap to imagine sin ;
   And blinding Truth half-bare unto his seeing.
It was the living man who had come in—
   Jonah's thoughts flying through his being.

Viola Meynell

THE FROZEN OCEAN

THE sea would flow no longer,
  It wearied after change,
It called its tides and breakers in,
  From where they might range.

It sent an icy message
  To every wave and rill;
They lagged, they paused, they stiffened,
  They froze, and were still.

It summoned in its currents,
  They reached not where they led;
It bound its foaming whirlpools.
  "Not the old life," it said,

"Not fishes for the fishermen,
  Not bold ships as before,
Not beating loud for ever
  Upon the seashore,

"But cold white foxes stepping
  On to my hard proud breast,
And a bird coming sweetly
  And building a nest.

Viola Meynell

" My icebergs shall be mountains,
    My silent fields of snow
Unmarked shall join the lands' snowfields—
    Where, no man shall know."

Richard Middleton
(1882–1911)

THE PRIZE

I WON you from the harsh intolerant sea
And made you into dreams, and never an hour
Passed into nothing but you came to me
With news of starry nights, and all the world
Thrilled, as with joy for summer buds unfurled,
For, lo! of every dream I made a flower.

Then lie at rest, O Love, and stir no more
In sombre worlds and grey. We have our
    dreams,
And God knows there were never dreamed
    before
Such dreams as these that on the untrodden hill
Of sleep make wonderful our lives, until
Over the sea the last pale planet gleams.

So there may an end, but loving here
There is no power in our mortal breath
That, being checked, our love may change to
    fear;
For we are only dreams and all our gold
Is dust of dreams. How may our love be cold
In this fair place though sleep were very death?

I won you from the harsh intolerant earth
To our high kingdom with the stars above,
Glad with fair things and radiant with Spring
    mirth.
And though beneath the world's unkindly sky
Our day shall pass, yes, though we surely die,
Fear not, I shall not lose you so, O Love!

TWO O'CLOCK IN THE MORNING

    In this quiet place
      I to sleep am fain;
    Sorrow hides her face
      And again
      Castle-lights of Spain
    Touch my life with grace.

    Though the world went wrong
      All my life ago,
    Here dear shadows throng,

And I know
  Summer has its snow
And my heart its song.

Be the darkness deep
  And let silence fill
All the starry steep:
  If God will
  When the world is still
I shall fall asleep.

Be it sleep or death.

Susan Miles
(1887–)

THE HARES

I

IMMOBILE, but fearless,
  With peace in her eyes,
The shy hare of friendship
  Scarce a yard from him lies.

He has stretched a swift hand
  To caress the free head.
The shy hare that was friendship
  To the covert has sped.

Susan Miles

II

The wild hare of love
  Is alert at his feet.
Oh, the fierce quivering heart!
  Oh, the heart's fierce beat!

He has tightened his noose.
  It was fine as a thread;
But the wild hare that was love
  At his feet lies dead.

Alice Milligan

(Living)

WHEN I WAS A LITTLE GIRL

WHEN I was a little girl,
  In a garden playing,
A thing was often said
  To chide us delaying:

When after sunny hours,
  At twilight's falling,
Down through the garden walks
  Came our old nurse calling.

[171]

"Come in! for it's growing late,
   And the grass will wet ye!
Come in! or when it's dark
   The Fenians will get ye."

Then, at this dreadful news,
   All helter-skelter,
The panic-struck little flock
   Ran home for shelter.

And round the nursery fire
   Sat still to listen,
Fifty bare toes on the hearth,
   Ten eyes a-glisten,

To hear of a night in March,
   And loyal folk waiting,
To see a great army of men
   Come devastating,

An army of Papists grim,
   With a green flag o'er them,
Red-coats and black police
   Flying before them.

But God (who our nurse declared
   Guards British Dominions)
Sent down a deep fall of snow
   And scattered the Fenians.

"But somewhere they're lurking yet,
    Maybe they're near us,"
Four little hearts pit-a-pat
    Thought, "Can they hear us?"

Then the wind-shaken pane
    Sounded like drumming;
"Oh!" they cried, "tuck us in,
    The Fenians are coming!"

Four little pairs of hands
    In the cots where she led those,
Over their frightened heads
    Pulled up the bedclothes.

But one little rebel there,
    Watching all with laughter,
Thought, "When the Fenians come
    I'll rise and go after."

Wished she had been a boy
    And a good deal older—
Able to walk for miles
    With a gun on her shoulder.

Able to lift aloft
    The Green Flag o'er them
(Red-coats and black police
    Flying before them).

And, as she dropped asleep,
  Was wondering whether
God, if they prayed to Him,
  Would give fine weather.

THE WAKE FEAST
(*A Young Girl Dead*)

Man of the house, soft-hearted with your
    sorrow,
  Woman of the house, with weeping near-hand
    blind,
Though I spoke ye fair the day and will again
    the morrow,
  It is no good wish for ye I have in my mind.

Young men, talking low on seats beside the
    doorway,
  Old men, drinking quietly on benches next
    the fire,
Great would be the fear and wonder would
    come o'er ye
  If I stood up among ye now and cried out
    my desire.

The desire of my heart to you, oh, people, it
    is cruel,
    Since I crossed the threshold where she is
        lying dead ;
She was my secret love, my hidden, shining
    jewel,
    And I would be glad the day if ye had died
        instead.

She was my secret love ; like a star afar I saw
    her,
    Or if out of sight, I was hoping for her still,
Looking from the field up the long roadway
    for her
    Till I saw the walk of her, head-shawled,
        down-hill.

Talk then of rain or any change of weather,
    Oh, she was quick in passing and I left to
        stand,
Being Donal of the Rosses, a boy hired to labour,
    And Sheelah the daughter on a farm of land.

Sealed are her lips now, the coffin here to hold
    her,
    If I ever learn now I have long to wait,
If she ever knew then the love I never told her
    As she went head-shawled, shyly by the gate.

Alice Milligan

A NOCTURNE

(In Memory of Marjorie MacDonald Arthur
Died at Derry High School, 1892)

On a night of sorrow I cried aloud her name.
God, who heard, said, "Hasten," and in my
  dream she came.
She stood; I saw her clearly by the moon's
  white flame;
Her eyes were sweet as ever; her voice was yet
  the same.

No illumining radiance lit her girlish brow—
As in life I loved her, I beheld her now;
I smiled in joy to greet her, nor did I think it
  strange
That death had wrought no change.

She bore with her no blossoms unknown to
  earthly land,
No tall, white flowers of paradise, stately and
  grand;
There were violets on her breast—blue violets—
And a red rose in her hand.

"How have you gathered?" I asked my gentle
    one,
"In that unchanging region of never-ceasing
    sun,
Where the March wind blows never, and no
    rain-shower ever wets,
Those little violets?"

"I have had them long," she said; "I have
    loved them much,
They were the last flowers given my living hands
    to touch,
And in the fevered night of pain before my
    death,
Sweet was the fragrance of their breath."

"But surely you have gathered in the celestial
    land
That other flower which lovingly is kept in
    your hand?
For there is not growing here on the mountain
    in the snows
Any such crimson rose?"

With looks of tenderest reproach my words
    were met.

M

" Dear, I have remembered! Dear, can you
    forget ?
Seaward, north of Derry, it fed on sun and dew ;
It was a gift from you.

" And I shall always treasure it as priceless in
    worth,
God has made nothing fairer than the little
    flowers of earth,
As He has no more to give in His Heaven above
Than your own heart's gift of never-changing
    love."

THE WHITE WAVE FOLLOWING

*(Written on a voyage through the Hebrides
In Memory of M. M. A.)*

Like the white wave following
Our ship through changing waters,
The memory of your love is
In life that alters :
The clouds pass overhead,
And like clouds the islands
Flock up—and hurrying on
Float by on the blue of the ocean ;
The sun goes, and the moon,
Along many mountains

Amid changing stars,
Into heaven uprolling,
New lochs and lands
In each hour illumines :
And all waves of the sea,
Tide-swept and wind-swayed
From morning unto night,
Move ceaselessly by us.

But against all winds
And all swift tide-races,
To all lochs and lands
And sea-girt lonely places,
Sunlit and moonlit,
Heaving and hollowing
Through wind-gleam, and glass-calm,
Comes one white wave following.

And like that white wave,
In the sunlit Sound of Jura,
Like that wave, bright-crested
Amid grey seas by Sanda,
On black rocks breaking
Around distant Rona,
Or in foam track fading
O'er a sea of slumber,
As we came from Canna

To Skye of your kindred :
Like that white wave, following
The ship through changing waters,
The memory of your love is
In life that alters.

A SONG OF FREEDOM

In Cavan of little lakes,
   As I was walking with the wind,
And no one seen beside me there, :
   There came a song into my mind :
It came as if the whispered voice
   Of one, but none of human kind,
Who walked with me in Cavan then,
   And he as invisible as wind.

On Urris of Inish-Owen,
   As I went up the mountain side,
The brook that came leaping down
   Cried to me—for joy it cried ;
And when from off the summit far
   I looked o'er land and water wide,
I was more joyous than the brook
   That met me on the mountain side.

To Ara of Connacht's isles,
    As I went sailing o'er the sea,
The wind's word, the brook's word,
    The wave's word, was plain to me—
" As we are, though she is not
    As we are, shall Banba be—
There is no King can rule the wind,
    There is no fetter for the sea."

FIONNUALA

AMONG the reeds round waters blue
    White wings are spread:
And she is seen, who should have been
    For centuries dead:
She, who ice-pierced in perilous coasts
    To land and sky
Lifted the swan-song of her grief
    Yet could not die.

Enchantment fell and powerful spell
    Of demon hate,
Had robbed her of her maiden robes,
    Her royal state.
And she, 'mid halls of kindred kind
    Might walk no more,
But floated far a phantom pale
    From shore to shore.

And yet the spell of demons fell
    Through ages long
Touched not the everlasting soul
    The power of song,
And they who mourn her bleeding breast
    And broken wing
Shall see her rise in beauty yet
    The child of the King.

Susan L. Mitchell
(1866–1926)

THE BUILDERS

THE jewelled word, the pillared phrase
    From the beleaguered heart are won.
Not without wounds her towers they raise
    Who come rebuilding Babylon.

We see the magic domes they build.
    The builder's conflict who can see ?
The hearts with grief and splendour filled
    Spoil of the sword of memory.

For other folk the day, the deed
    Unhymned may pass.   No slaver's whip
Scourges their pain to song, no reed
    Is pressed against the writhing lip.

Susan L. Mitchell

Round us the piteous ruins fall,
   Down in the dust defeated lie
Ilion and Emain Macha, all
   The kingly-hearted set so high.

From what dark hour the singer knew
   Came they, the anguish and the power—
Winged words that to high cities grew?
   Who sings the song rebuilds the tower.

Harold Monro
(1879–1932)

BLURRED ETCHING

INCREDIBLE. So near to paradise.
Time; Death: halt! Oh, what gardener has
  been here?
Are the trees conscious? Are they, even, wise?
Do they know Adam when he wanders near?
He touches them. They answer through the
    lake.
They love the wind that leans to comb their
    leaves.
(When a bird sings, then all its feathers shake.)
And yet when Adam thinks the garden grieves.

[183]

He should not give unconsciousness a name.
No sound. Low wind. Still water . . . Then
 a man
Under the weeping willow roughly came,
And idly kicked an empty old tin can
Into the lake, but only to the fright
Of one lank swan who wanders, lonely, white.

T. Sturge Moore
(1870–1944)

SEEN IN THE PARK

I MEETING her, for unassumèd pride,
For irreproachable beauty, for calm health,
Thought I saw Cleopatra live again.
She was not naked but was clothed as one
On whom a robe is needless for defence ;
If for adornment, wholly vain : I felt
Delight in men advance warm through her gaze,
Though nothing that sought friendship of a
 soul ;
But as a child well-pleased to front a lion,
Being brave of heart, she gazed on handsome
 males ;

[184]

And as a princely child disdains to snatch
Though it have appetite, she without greed
Surveyed each stalwart form with leisured
    pause
Whose estimate of Anthony and Cæsar
Has since received endorsement from the world:
Those brows assumed that history would yield
That echo of their judgment, which is fame.

A TRAGIC FATE

She was a woman, knew her face surpassed her
    In all perfections to its nature free;
Yet dared she ever, to buy off disaster,
    Lavish her soul in laughter slavishly.

Nor in rank mirth alone, the queen dissembling,
    Her beauty mocked its sov'rainty and pride;
But large feigned tears must cross her wan
    cheeks, trembling
    Pretenders to the passion she'ld deride.

Yea joy and grief, like goddesses apparelled,
    Did menial service for her sordid fears:
Motives with which all dignity had quarrelled,
    Ravished with elfin tones most prudent ears.

To meet the moment's pressure any master
  Might watch, admire, possess, if he could pay ;
The soul accepted what he, sated, cast her,
  And gave the body's grand reserve away.

Ah ! taxed by age, to death needs-be delivered,
  Its glorious aspects wasted to vile ends,
Hopelessly subject until wholly withered,
  Where shall the outraged body seek amends ?

LEGLESS

"And legless birds of Paradise"—Keats's reference to a
popular error.

THOU perfect mock, Thou beauty,
Endue our clay with grief !
Could flesh acquire duty
Were heartache not a thief ?
Although fair form be dumb
Whence else can rapture come ?
A consonance from dove-tailed shapes
Like started hare escapes . . .

Nay, pinioned to aspire,
Footless to scorn the mire,
A torch-flap of that fire
About the night dispersed,
Is beauty, coursed and coursing, so cursing, so
    accursed.

On, on, her flight devours
An endless file of hours !
Pursuit reaps no requiting
There lacks her for alighting
Leg, claw and grip . .
A gaudy ship,
Havenless she floats in air,
And hearts grow sick, she tacks so wide and
    luffs so fair !

Trim, trim, antennae gleaming,
The coquet toy,
Far swept with soundless swish
O'er gloom sequestered fish,
Angles for joy . .
All feel they must be dreaming,
Watch that and nought beside
Cross the unbounded, the unfathomed, the
    unillumined tide,
Leaving in the darkness
Our longing to its starkness.

—Man, over leagues of jumbled impenetrable
    forest
Flitteth what thou adorest ;
Then thy sore need grows sorest.

Yet, once or twice, like angel,
She stoops down t'ward a pool;
Flames roaring to estrange all
The still, the mute, the cool..
Then wavers, circles, pulses
Retrieving rash descent,
Hovers and convulses,
While flowing plumes back bent
Wreathe gorgeous like a rose
About an intense core,
Purpose lapsed!.. yet soon anew her fate
    she knows
Darts downward as before..
Ah! not with power of healing,
But with excess of feeling,
Both courting and revealing
Herself in an abyss.

Responsive to such kindness,
Comrade for headlong rapture,
Rises from depths of blindness
A prey who hopes to capture,
To woo, to kiss.

Twain, all but one they near
Mutually waxing dear!
Eyes, big with image clear,

Fashion the best to be,
Fusion and ecstasy
Of heart in heart!

Truth dawns, they start;
Then, equally wronged, part, part!
One retreats o'er tree-tops far
Mounts, dwindles, grows a star:
What gulfs those black depths are
To quench that other
Neither mate nor brother,
Without connection
A mere reflection!

Bravely winged from Paradise
Promise stooped, but promise lies!
A bird so incomplete
Lacking both legs and feet
Can neither tread nor yet be trod,
In imitation of the god
Projecting on unending line
Beings fine and superfine.

Yes, a sheer mock is beauty
Endowing clay with grief!
Had flesh conceived of duty
Were heartache not a thief

Robbing the nameless, the unknown
Of kindness and conception?
A bodiless coupling blind and dumb
Whence
Many perfect numbers come;
From consonance of dream-denatured shapes
Melody escapes.
Hence,
Occurrence wholly odd,
Which pairs with nothing ruled by law
But braves the world mechanic and its god..
Causes that pain which brings love awe..
Incalculable, yet can wed with hope
For which the universe yields nowhere scope. .
And, cramped in light's house, feels compelled
    to grope
Disdaining sideral islands which men learn
With instruments to number and discern:
Here is an alien immaterial kind
Not to be likened unto aught, save mind!

Thomas Moult
(1890–   )

THE TWO WATCHERS

The south air swings the cowslips
  Over the autumn floor;
An apple from the bough slips
  Ripe-russet to the core.
Across the yellow dazzle, like a white drifting
      feather,
I watch my white love wander, the fallen fruit
      to gather.

I watch my white love looting
  Quietly, the season's sweet.
And a blackbird watches, fluting
  With each lithe stoop for beat.
Over the yellow dazzle his measure thrills
      loud-throated:
Hushed, in my heart's deep, thrills a wonder
      golden-noted.

Seumas O'Sullivan

(1879–   )

THE TWILIGHT PEOPLE

It is a whisper among the hazel bushes ;
　It is a long, low, whispering voice that fills
With a sad music the bending and swaying
　　　rushes ;
　It is a heart-beat deep in the quiet hills.

Twilight people, why will you still be crying,
　Crying and calling to me out of the trees ?
For under the quiet grass the wise are lying,
　And all the strong ones are gone over the seas.

And I am old, and in my heart at your calling
　Only the old dead dreams a-fluttering go,
As the wind, the forest wind, in its falling
　Sets the withered leaves fluttering to and fro.

THE SEDGES

I whispered my great sorrow
　To every listening sedge ;
And they bent, bowed with my sorrow,
　Down to the water's edge.

[192]

But she stands and laughs lightly
　　To see me sorrow so,
Like the light winds that laughing
　　Across the water go.

If I could tell the bright ones
　　That quiet-hearted move,
They would bend down like the sedges
　　With the sorrow of love.

But she stands laughing lightly,
　　Who all my sorrow knows,
Like the little wind that laughing
　　Across the water blows.

PRAISE

Dear, they are praising your beauty,
　　The grass and the sky:
The sky in a silence of wonder,
　　The grass in a sigh.

I too would sing for your praising,
　　Dearest, had I
Speech as the whispering grass,
　　Or the silent sky.

[193]

These have an art for the praising
  Beauty so high.
Sweet, you are praised in a silence,
  Sung in a sigh.

CYGNETS ON THE CANAL

PROUDLY the young swans breast
The green wind-roughened water,
And through their brown-grey feathers
Take, delicious, the cool east.
O not through brown-grey feathers only,
But through the city, and through all its ways
Blow, purifying east.

Herbert Palmer
(1880–   )

IN AUTUMN
(An Ode)

IN Autumn the last fruits turn mellow,
And many flowers flaunt yellow,
And brown and russet-yellow are the hill-places
That the winds haunt.

And as dripping nights daunt the sun's lights
The famished leaves flutter yellow
Round the trees growing gaunt.

Autumn is a brown and yellow time
Soon after life's prime,
The time of a knell
Of everything man loved too well—
When from some dim belfry of starshine
The gold and brassy bells of Change
Utter mournful ding-dongs
To the changing sing-songs
Crying, sighing where the grasses shone,
" It is all all over,
The leaping of life is over,
The cherry and the clover are gone."

Very strangely the music flows,
And the woof across the warp dims and glows—
Brown and yellow with a glint of rose.

But the soul of man grieves;
And thick as whirled leaves
While tired Time weaves
This third of his mysteries
The birds crowd in the aching trees
And where late stood the corn-sheaves.

[195]

How the birds twitter and complain.
How they complain to the creeping grey rain !

And yet near the heart of the weeping there is
    mirth ;
For many days laugh with the joy of the sun
And the hued brightness of Earth
That recks not Death's whiteness.

And bridal seem the stubble field-ways
When crowned with a coronal of tinted weeds
And blackberry beads
Decay pipes sweetly on her Pan-reeds ;

Or dances full of amaze,
Heavy garlanded with the red berries
(Redder than the farm cherries)
From the hedge that the bright sun bleeds
And the Night slays
With her blanket of haze.

Then, though man scarce heeds,
Out of the west a finger beckons,
Westward beckons—
Some strange allure
That throbs in the heart of all Change.

Herbert Palmer

Very strange and pure are the days
When the bright sun through a silver haze
Steals slowly into a zenith of blue.

And you and I, I and you
Stand as if on the brink of Spring
Listening,
Wondering.

For strange lovers walk softly in the field-ways
As the sky falters and the wind sways.

And the ageing man turns a flushed face to the
       green girl,
Saying in a low tone that shudders to the wind's
       moan,
" Look ! how lovely there where the tossed
       leaves whirl !
Is it not good that something is lost ? "

And yet it is only Death that cometh
With his sickle of frost
And his diadem of snow-pearl.

BROOK NOSTALGIA

OH, I would go away and fire my eyes,
Get a new brain, and woo the gravel flies,
And make a glow-worm pillow of my sighs!

Forget, forget—where alder roots cling wet.
Where water runs I can a year forget.
The empty brain grows pleasuring ears and eyes.

See, watch, suspend. Just that, and gild my
    nose,
Mindless as hern or otter, in the sun's throes,
Where rock-moss drips, where water gleams
    and flows.

Grey is my heart, and grey the face of thee.
These chopine heels set not the pace for me.
Where winds walk warily I cannot see.

But by the ivied bridge the dun-flies gleam;
The brown trout turns his speckles to the
    stream,
And small stones stun my dark street-troubled
    dream.

Only where water runs I can forget.
Fins, little wings and pebbles pearl Time's net.
What sometimes was, came oft, and shall be yet.

Herbert Palmer

CHRISTMAS MINIATURE

I SEE a great white space, in the midst of it
        Christmas,
    A shrine of coloured candles on the King's
        highway;
And He who sits in state is our own quiet Jesus,
    And she who lights the tallow-wicks, May.

For Mary hath her roses and bluebells in
        December,
    All dewy is her gown with the Spring.
I see it so plain in the Yuletide ember,
    Round her the merry birds sing;

One of them has feathers like a little yellow-
        hammer,
    One of them is azure as the day;
And a green thrush hops on a white woolly
        lamb;
    While round them the angels play

On sackbut and psaltery and castanets,
    On tibia and tambourine and lyre.
And seven little alabaster minarets
    See I, too, in the forest of the fire.

[199]

Herbert Palmer

DEIRDRE'S AGONY

GONE! Gone! gone away! Far, far, far
  away!
  Wait for ever where the moonlight falls.
O my mouth, still thy moans! Break heart, on
  the stones!
  Wail thy sorrow where the wild cat calls.

Rack me, tempests! be my bier; carry me afar
  from here!
  Trample on me, Darkness, ere the fires burn
  low!
Weep ye wolves, if ye have eyes! See my lion
  where he lies,
  Lifeless beneath his shield—cold as the snow.

Woven starlight was his mind. Ye, so envious
  and blind,
  Dark slavish cruel lords will rue it to the
  tomb.
He was swifter than the fawn, bright of body as
  the dawn,
  Braver than a lion. Oh! ye hands of doom.

Whirl my limbs against the trees for your
    coward King to seize,
  Point his spear to my heart; draw your lean
    traitor swords.
He shall ache in curtained gloom for my breasts
    beneath the tomb;
  I will never soothe his pillow. Ye have
    slain the lord of lords,—

A god above ye seven—Where art thou, Thews
    of Heaven?
  Oh! the temple star is fallen, silent are the
    walls.
Vanity of vanities! Fled are all the sanities.
  Come to me Great Spirit ere the dawn-cock
    calls!

HEAVEN

When I am dead and transported and under
    the ground,
Wrapped by walls that are soundless, out of
    Earth's centre and round,
One joy will be mine that none of the living
    shall share,
For I shall be perfectly quiet as I lie there.

Herbert Palmer

Oh! Life will be soundless, though deluged
    with essence of sound,
Shut in walls that are groundless, though reared
    to us out of the ground.
And the noisy shall know and repent where no
    life jars,
Where the hush of the flowers is blent with the
    chime of the stars.

And a hundred pitying glow-worms shining low,
And a thousand quickening angels, row on row,
Will point in the Book of Life, whose leaves
    are seven,
That Heaven is Quiet and the soul has peace
    in Heaven.

Eden Phillpotts

(1862–   )

LITANY TO PAN

By the abortions of the teeming Spring,
By Summer's starved and withered offering,
By Autumn's stricken hope and Winter's sting,
Oh, hear!

By the ichneumon on the writhing worm,
By the swift far-flung poison of the germ,

By soft and foul brought out of hard and firm,
Oh, hear !

By the fierce battle under every blade,
By the etiolation of the shade,
By drought and thirst and things undone, half made,
Oh, hear !

By all the horrors of re-quickened dust,
By the eternal waste of baffled lust,
By mildews and by cankers and by rust,
Oh, hear !

By the fierce scythe of Spring upon the wold,
By the dead eaning mother in the fold,
By stillborn stricken young and tortured old,
Oh, hear !

By fading eyes pecked from a dying head,
By the hot mouthful of a thing not dead,
By all thy bleeding, struggling, shrieking red,
Oh, hear !

By all the agonies of all the past,
By earth's cold dust and ashes at the last,
By her return to the unconscious vast,
Oh, hear !

FELINE ANYWAY

"LIFE'S a cat with nine sharp tails:"
Loud laments the man who fails.
"Life's a cat with nine good lives,"
Answers him the man who thrives.
Good or ill their fate may be,
Life's a cat they both agree;
Let what fortune haunt the house,
Life's a cat and man's a mouse.

THE WASP

A SEVERED wasp yet drank the juice
Of a ripe pear upon a plate,
And one did idly meditate
What was the use.

Yet round about us, spent and done,
With hands already growing cold,
We see half-men still scraping gold,
Its uses gone.

Eden Phillpotts

THE FAIR

THE fair is a fight; some are fighting for gain;
Some fighting for pleasure and some to cheat
    pain;
But that squinting old hag, with a voice like a
    knife
And a tray of wire spiders—she's fighting for
    life.

THE WIFE

WE murmured of his kindliness
When by his pit a hundred stood;
We held him loyal, generous, good,
And only spoke his name to bless.

But, when three years and more were sped,
I came again beside his grave,
And found red dock and darnel wave
Above the unrecorded dead.

His widow listened to my plea,
Then made reply in smouldering tone:
" My master froze my heart to stone;
That's all the stone he'll get from me!"

Eden Phillpotts

THE OLD SINGER

HE came to sing some olden songs
That hardly any now remember.
He braved a night of wild December
And tramped in pregnant with his wrongs.

He grumbled at his weight of years
And cursed the harsh, unfriendly season;
He offered a sufficient reason
Why future time for him meant tears.

Yet, when the wight began to sing
An ancient Carolean ditty,
He asked for no man's ruth, or pity,
But made the cottage dresser ring.

The song for him wove passing sleight
To summon churchyard folk together,
Helped him forget his slender tether
And woke a laugh that winter night.

His far-off look and far-off smile
Welcomed dead men and women, stealing
With some faint, ghostly power of healing,
To hearten him a little while.

Ruth Pitter

(1897–   )

THE CONSUMMATION

(1918)

Looks royal, songs for heaven meet,
  Thou wishest, thinking on his worth
Whose faintest image is more sweet
  Than all thy dearest loves on earth.

The royal look is marred with years,
  The song celestial is made
Into a litany of tears,
  Into a blossom of the shade.

Thou art fordone : thine heart is rent
  To praise who hath no fear nor shame,
Yet when thine utmost life is spent
  Thou hast not even said his name :

But peace, the triumph is not ripe.
  Canst thou not sleep a little space
Or dream upon the oaten pipe
  Till there appear the only face ?

Then well sufficing shall arise
  From thy quiet heart that was so wrung,
A look in those translated eyes,
  A word in that diviner tongue.

Ruth Pitter

IN PRAISE
(1919)

O SING of all thy saints, friend Poesy,
Thy company incomparable hymn forth:
Mute in the mortal voice, but tuneable,
Most tuneable, where all beside is death;
Fluting in winds and praying in still airs,
Missalled in flowers and merry in green leaves.
Sweetly shall I be shriven of weariness
And rest, rest, rest—and yet be large in life
If thou extend one fold of thine apparel
For silken mail, bright harness marvellous.
Send me not forth; for I am loath to go;
I am fidelity that still abideth
Both poor and gentle in all righteousness
And keeps the door, both for to hearken thee,
And through the wicket call to wayfarers
Like throstle in cold harbourage of spring,
Some notes of thee, with bright eye and still
    plume
And passionate throat, and never a thought but
    song.
I will not count the dawns nor the moon's
    wanings,
Nor see the errant tides dance up the strand,
Unless it chance thou sing of the new day,

Or of stars gathered in the golden sickle,
Or the upleaping wild and fairy wave.
Call war, I am a legion; stay at home,
Sing lullaby to babes, and so will I.
Play with a blade of grass, 'tis beautiful;
Or rive the forest like a wind from hell,
Still will I follow and that cheerfully.
And Heaven shall smile that I forget my soul,
And frown not; for thy silver traffickings
Are thorough Heaven, where I shall light me
    down
When that thou stayest, and the world is burned.

SILENCE SHALL COVER THEE
(1919)

SILENCE shall cover thee; the dark
    Shall wrap thee from the curious sun;
Thy monuments of sorrow stark
    Weather and crumble one by one.

Hunger meets weariness in thee,
    And penury their hands doth join;
The yellow flower beneath the tree
    But mocks thee, like a golden coin.

[209]

O

Yet but one mother have ye twain;
   The earth that chides the flower with death,
And mourns thee with a summer rain,
   And in her mantle harboureth.

Long are the dreams of earth; thy grief
   Is like shrill gnats in lovely eves,
Or like one early-withered leaf
   When every herb is dark with leaves.

The lute nor the high trumpet sings
   To thee whose only wealth is peace:
Thine the meek linnet's sober wings,
   Thy robe is of the humble fleece.

TO LYRIC POETRY
(1921)

WHAT has evoked thee, nymph of the fresh
    groves?
Some passing warmth in a November heart,
Some gleam? I called thee not, but there thou
    art,
Attended by thy few and pensive Loves,
And shining through the wilderness apart:

Pacing like silver through a silvan shade,
Or toiling on the highway close behind
My care-weighed steps, and withering in the
    wind,
Dear love, fond fragile warrior, wilful maid !
It is for thee I call the air unkind.

It is for thee that I deem cheerfulness
A wanton noise, and hate simplicity
For that she thoughtless is, and rustic-free,
And hath no care to please thee in her dress,
And laughs, and passes by, and shoulders thee.

And wert thou tempted out of solitude
By the untimely summer of my thought ?
Hast thou no palaces of green boughs wrought,
No friend than all this company less rude,
Have all thy leafy shrines then fallen to naught ?

Go under ground, thou gentlest flower, retire !
Bow thy blest head, cover thyself with leaves ;
Ere I was born they had housed all the sheaves,
And closed the door, and tended on the fire,
And hid the blunted sickle in the eaves.

LET ME NOT LIVE
(1922)

LET me not live in a sad monument,
    But let me be
Far from the searching of remembrance sent,
    Sunk in the sea;
The Gods have written death; set not to time
    The trifling bound
Of marble, nor a tablet marred with rhyme,
    No plot of ground;
I was less fair than clouds, and no man makes
    Statues to these;
Forget me; think upon the silent lakes,
    The slender trees.

FIDELE
(1924)

LAMENT thee? yea, I'll weep,
    Though I weep none;
Soft, soft be thy sleep,
    Imagined one!
How fair the daisied grass
    Grows in the mind!
And that which never was
    Most fair I find.

Shepherd, how did she look?
  O bonny, O white!
Then in this loved book
  She shall give light;
The winter holds the wood,
  Cold is the rain;
But I seek flowers in my mood
  Never in vain.

Lament thee? yea, I'll sigh
  Morning and eve,
Though for no other I
  Am known to grieve.
In my own way and tongue
  I'll mourn and bless thee,
And the dim garland of my song
  Will not oppress thee.

Max Plowman
(1883–1941)

HER BEAUTY

I HEARD them say, "Her hands are hard as
    stone,"
And I remembered how she laid for me

The road to heaven. They said, " Her hair
   is grey."
Then I remembered how she once had thrown
Long plaited strands, like cables, into the sea
I battled in—the salt sea of dismay.
They said, " Her beauty's past." And then I
   wept,
That these, who should have been in love adept,
Against my fount of beauty should blaspheme,
And hearing a new music, miss the theme.

Sir Arthur Quiller-Couch

(1863–1944)

SHADOWS

As I walked out on Hallows' E'en,
I saw the moon swing thin and green ;
I saw beside, in Fiddler's Wynd,
Two hands that moved upon a blind.

As I walked out on Martin's Feast,
I heard a woman say to a priest—
" His grave is digged, his shroud is sewn ;
And the child shall pass for his very own."

But whiles they stood beside his tomb,
I heard the babe laugh out in her womb—
" My hair will be black as his was red,
And I have a mole where his heart bled."

T. W. Ramsey
(1892–   )

IMAGO

A SIN is a small and delicate thing
　　At first; it scarcely raises its head;
It creeps where the dust and shadows cling;
　　It fears the heel that may bruise and tread.

And then the swift metamorphosis,
　　Out of sound, out of sight,
From larva to hard, cold chrysalis—
　　And then the winged, silent thing bold in
　　　　the light!

The great soft moth that doth confound
　　—So fair and delicate to see!—
And in corruption bring to ground
　　Strength, wisdom and integrity.

T. W. Ramsey

TRIADS

THREE things too frail
To be touched without spoiling:
The bloom on the grape,
The snow-petal pale,
The thin web the toiling,
Precise spiders shape.

Three things too wide
For conception to span:
The intricate courses
On which the stars ride,
Life's hidden forces,
The profound heart of man.

Ernest Rhys
(1859–1946)

AN AUTOBIOGRAPHY

WALES England wed; so I was bred. 'Twas
  merry London gave me breath.
I dreamt of love, and fame: I strove. But
  Ireland taught me love was best:

And Irish eyes, and London cries, and streams of
  Wales, may tell the rest.
What more than these I asked of Life, I am
  content to have from Death.

Caron Rock
(1884–   )

HE IS THE LONELY GREATNESS

HE IS the lonely greatness of the world—
      (His eyes are dim),
His power it is holds up the Cross
      That holds up Him.

He takes the sorrow of the threefold hour—
      (His eyelids close),
Round Him and round, the wind—His Spirit—
  where
      It listeth blows.

And so the wounded greatness of the world
      In silence lies—
And death is shattered by the light from out
      Those darkened eyes.

T. W. Rolleston
(1857–1920)

CLONMACNOISE
(From the Irish of Angus O'Gillan)

IN a quiet water'd land, a land of roses,
　　Stands Saint Kieran's city fair;
And the warriors of Erin in their famous
　　　　generations
　　Slumber there.

There beneath the dewy hillside sleep the
　　　　noblest
　　Of the clan of Conn,
Each below his stone with name in branching
　　　　Ogham
　　And the sacred knot thereon.

There they laid to rest the seven Kings of Tara,
　　There the sons of Cairbrè sleep—
Battle-banners of the Gael that in Kieran's
　　　　plain of crosses
　　Now their final hosting keep.

And in Clonmacnoise they laid the men of
　　　　Teffia,
　　And right many a lord of Breagh;
Deep in sod above Clan Creidè and Clan Conaill,
　　Kind in hall and fierce in fray.

T. W. Rolleston

Many and many a son of Conn the Hundred-
        fighter
    In the red earth lies at rest;
Many a blue eye of Clan Colman the turf covers,
    Many a swan-white breast.

Ethel Rolt-Wheeler
(1869–   )

THE ALMOND TREE

SHE thrills to waking in her Winter tomb,
Her swaddling bands unloosen, bond by bond,
She knows the Spring her lover waits beyond,
Impetuous radiance fills her narrow room:
She hears his step above the muffled boom
Of bursting pod, the crisping of the frond,
The push of catkins in the hazel-wand,—
And all her being flutters into bloom.

Lady Margaret Sackville

(1881–   )

TO ONE WHO DENIES

Old friend, I greet you! you are still the same:
You poisoned Socrates, you crucified
Christ, you have persecuted, mocked, denied,
Rejected God and cursed Him—in God's name.
You gave monotonously to the flame
All those (whom now you honour) when the
    new
Truth stung their lips—for fear it might be true;
Then reaped where they had sown, and felt
    no shame.

Familiar voice, old adversary—hail!
Yesterday's fools are now your gods. Behold!
The generations pass and we can wait.
You slandered Pasteur, Florence Nightingale;
Now a new splendour quivers in the cold
Grey shadows overhead; *still* you are late.

The Hon. V. Sackville-West
(1892–   )

THE ISLAND

She walks among the loveliness she made,
Between the apple-blossom and the water—
She walks among the patterned pied brocade,
Each flower her son, and every tree her daughter.
This is an island all with flowers inlaid,
A square of grassy pavement tessellated ;
Flowers in their order blowing as she bade,
And in their company by her created.
The waving grasses freckle sun with shade,
The wind-blown waters round the kingcups
    ripple,
Colour on colour chequered and arrayed,
Shadow on light in variable stipple.
Her regiments at her command parade,
Foot-soldier primrose in his rank comes trooping,
Then wind-flowers in a scarlet loose brigade,
Fritillary with dusky orchis grouping.
They are the Cossacks, dim in ambuscade,
Scarfed in their purple like a foreign stranger,
Piratical, and apt for stealthy raid,
Wherever's mystery or doubtful danger.
Iris salutes her with his broad green blade,
And marches by with proud imperial pennant,

And tulips in a flying cavalcade
Follow valerian for their lieutenant.
The lords-and-ladies dressed for masquerade
In green silk domino discreetly hooded,
Hurry towards the nut-trees' colonnade,
Philandering where privacy's well wooded;
They're the civilians of this bold crusade,
The courtiers of this camp by blossom tented,
With woodbine clambering the balustrade,
And all by briar roses battlemented.
There, in the sunlit grasses green as jade,
She walks; she sees her squadrons at attention,
And, laughing at her flowery escapade,
Stretches her hands towards her dear invention.

Siegfried Sassoon
(1886–   )

AT THE GRAVE OF HENRY VAUGHAN

ABOVE the voiceful windings of a river
An old green slab of simply graven stone
Shuns notice, overshadowed by a yew.
Here Vaughan lies dead, whose name flows on for ever
  for ever
Through pastures of the spirit washed with dew
And starlit with eternities unknown.

Siegfried Sassoon

Here sleeps the Silurist; the loved physician;
The face that left no portraiture behind;
The skull that housed white angels and had
    vision
Of daybreak through the gateways of the mind.
    Here faith and mercy, wisdom and humility
    (Whose influence shall prevail for evermore)
    Shine. And this lowly grave tells Heaven's
      tranquillity.
    And here stand I, a suppliant at the door.

Michael Scot
(1891–   )

THE LITTLE BLACK ASS

Poor woman, the pleasure of God
    Be over your way!
A blessing, O son, on the sod
    You were cutting to-day.

There was no one a moment before
    On your share of the ground.
I stepped up the rise of the shore
    And you looking around.

[223]

Michael Scot

And is it a tinker you are,
  Or a woman of charms?
And is it a child or a star
  That you have in your arms?

Is there hunger upon you who brood
  By this raggedy thorn?
I am trudging the wide earth for food
  Since the ring of the morn!

I will give you the apple I stole
  O'er the crown of a wall.
(Oh, bright in his eyes is the soul
  Of the child in your shawl!)

My spirit is lifted to reach
  This mountainy strand,
You are strange in the land by your speech?
  I am strange in the land.

Oh, the wounds of your walking are red
  On the dark of the turf!
From the roads of the East I have fled
  O'er the ridge of the surf.

And I hear a bell ringing for Mass,
   But scourged are my heels :
Oh, lend me the little black ass
   With the turf in his creels !

I will give you the ass for your steed
   Through wide Innisfail ;
No ass is his equal for speed
   In the land of the Gael.

He has travelled the bog, he is grey
   With the mist of the road,
But joy will be on him to-day
   With a queen for his load.

Oh, mount him, poor woman of light,
   Ere the chapel bell cease,
That his sleep may be lucky to-night
   And his wisdom increase !

I will mount him, O little green bough
   Of the tree of the West ;
Thine ass has a star on his brow
   And a cross on his breast.

P

M. P. Shiel
(1865–1947)

SONG OF THE COCK

COMING's the glory! Let me be throating,
Throwing my crow up, " Doesn't it grow, O!"
(Glum in the gloaming must I be mourning
    " Doesn't it go, O!")

Much like that bird which, purged by being
    burnt up,
Purpler resurges, 'verts he to earth up,
Something within him lurking, that works him,
    Bursts in rebirth up.

Would I could know him! find if his beaming
Merely be seeming, eyeing him nigh, O,
If he be realty, if he be dreaming:
    Would I could fly, O!

But he was fathered far from my askings,
And he is faster far than the dart is,
And there's a darkness hid in his ardour,
    In where his heart is.

Let me not question: I am a noodle,
Pecking a newt's head: let me be hooting,
Poking my neck out, puking the tooting,
    " Toodle de Loodle."

Easy my beak-holes! seeking no secrets:
See I it really, see I it dreaming,
Have I not reason, breathing these breezes,
 Screams to be screaming?

Claps for this palace! tapestries prank it,
Lazulites, scarlets, large is its arching,
Pageant of banners, bladder of phantoms,
 Charmed is it marching.

Blest be its Heart, His manners and customs:
Vapours ascend, an influence takes them,
Raindrops descend, an influence breaks them:
 Blest be what makes them.

Trim as a brick I! cinnabar crimson!
Hen-pecked this hill-top whither I've led them;
Wing-tip I lower, tripping love-dizzy,
 Threating to tread them.

Rosy corona, shall I not glory?
Throwing my crow up, "Doesn't it grow, O?"
(Glum in the gloaming must I be mourning
 "Doesn't it go, O!")

This is my morning; never was dawning
Born to *this* vesture; never shall dawning,
Daubed with *this* gesture, flaunt *this* adorning:
 This is my morning.

When it is frayed out, seraphs may sorrow,
Reft of its strangeness, ranging the Ages,
Wanting it, aching: *I* may be making
    Cock-broth to-morrow.

Now is my hour, my dower, my bower,
Yea, though I perish soon by the butcher,
Spray on his apron plash of death passion,
    Now is my flower.

Shouts for my hour! How shall I spend it?
Michael am I not, yet of the mighty:
Chyle's in my chyle-ducts, light's in my eye-
    stuff—
    Flyer than flighty!

Smith hath not hinged me, Titian tinged me:
Ages on ages raged He to raise me:
Peck I a cherry, angel, archangel,
    Cannot appraise me.

What is my name? "I AM" has He named
    me:
With him I stand—a Thing—in a star-knot:
Trash of tiaras, ravishing rajahs,
    Starrier are not.

M. P. Shiel

"IS" is my name, and "HIS" is my pet-name;
Nicknamed "UNIQUENESS," "HOSTS" is
    my state-name:
One of my toes being (blood-drop being billions)
    Trillions of trillions.

Nothing's above me borne in His bundle,
Zone beyond zone His zodiacs fold me:
Flew I to Beulah, homed in Boötes,
    Still would He hold me.

Oh, that my eyes were fountains of water,
That I might spout them all on this Altar,
Bowed, yet exalted, bound in His Order,
    Sound of His Psalter.

So I will spend it complexly-simply,
Pecking and sipping, miracles living,
Sips sacramental, sip, then a glance up,
    Sips with thanksgiving;

Summing my suns up, miserly, mindful,
Knowing that suns are sons of some mother:
Somewhere some sun has smouldered to light
    this:
    This will some other.

Down in the fowl-house, when he deserts us,
Mouse-mum I frower, lest he revert not,
Nervous, uncertain, certain that some day
    Sun-sperm will spurt not.

All this embroider, cloth of enjoyment,
Voyaging bauble buoyed on the void up,
Clotting, evolving, coiling to alter,
    Toils but to falter.

Groans, if its glory folks be not throating,
Throwing their crow up, " Doesn't it grow, O ! "
(Glum in its glooming some must be mourning
    " Doesn't it go, O ! ")

              *

Horace Shipp
(1891–   )

THE SIXTH DAY

*And God said, " Let us make man in our image, and
let him have dominion " . . .*

GOD made you in His image, yet I saw
you stoop and seize a blind mole from the snare.
Blind.
Blind with terror . . . blind.

Your teeth gleamed bare behind the taut, white
    lips.
The trapper's law knows neither hate nor love.
You watched it paw,
frantic with lust of life, the yielding air,
and were amused.
God's Image !
Did you care, pitying one moment, see the
    swift hands claw
for life and darkness, know and hate your trap ?
I saw your knuckles gleam, your hand swing
    free ;
a cry ;
the blind face crashed against a wall.
Then death and stillness, and—
you grinned.

Mayhap,
snaring the blind mole of humanity,
God made you in His image after all.

EVEREST
(To All who Explore New Paths)

WHAT went you forth to find ?
What new thing would you know ?

What secret read in the Mother of Mountain's
      blind,
blind eyes? What learn at her barren bosom
      of snow?

For what new thing should men
so strive, so agonise?
Is there some wonder in the remoteness beyond
      our ken;
some beauty; some wisdom beyond the dream
      of the wise?

Nay, not for that we strove,
nor any new thing found;
but this truth, ancient and everlasting, did we prove,
this beauty, this wisdom, on the high untrodden
*   ground;*

that where the safe ways end,
known and unknown divide,
God's great uncharted passes upward tend,
and the spirit of man undaunted is undenied;
and beyond the last camp-fire man has Faith for friend,
and beyond all guidance the courage of God for guide.

Edith Sitwell

(1887–   )

IN SPRING
(To Fytton Armstrong)

IN the silent kitchen
  The boards said, "It is Spring—
You will not find the cook, that witch, in—
  She has gone to hear woods sing."

The boards that were so dry and dead,
  They seemed the ghost's last bed,
Put forth one humble small green flower
  Of sunlight, shrill, unripe, and sour.

The lonely ghost then put one foot—
  One sad foot before the other—
"My old root pulls me, Death, my root—
  I only know the dust will smother

Me." Boards quacked like any duck
  Before the ghost's foot as it creaked.
"Believe then in the Spring's warm luck."
  Dust raised its snout to him, and squeaked.

For in the dreaming warm spring weather
   Much was stirring, waking then—
Not only life of fur or feather
   And the worlds long known of men.

The Cook forgot that huntsmen snare
   For man, his brother the small hare:
The lame and lonely Dark forgot
   How, hungry, it must snare and plot.

Then kind dust covered the ghost's bones
   As duck-quacking cold streams their stones,
And the floor-boards helped him then
   To pull his roots free, pitying men.

And outside in the warm spring weather,
   Humble creatures, glad together,
Creatures that when he was living
   He had hunted, snared, forgiving

Cried: " We'll warm with fur and feather
   Your cold heart, our lonely brother—
For we are brothers, once again
   Since you were snared and knew Death's
     pain."

Lewis Spence
(1874–   )

BRIDE OR HANDMAIDEN?

BEAUTY ever was designed
To thrill the heart and not the mind,
To speak to the immediate blood,
But never to the pensive mood.

And when I hear one say that thought
Has been to him by Beauty brought
I know that Beauty in his house
Has dwelt as servant, not as spouse.

Edward Storer
(1882–   )

THE YOUNG BRIDE

I AM seventeen, and they have given
  Me unto a man of twenty-nine.
He is very strong and lovely;
  He is mine.

I can fancy that the moon is
  Somehow stooping from the sky;
I should like to reach and kiss her—
  Ah! so happy I.

I am hungry, I am thirsty,
　　Yet I will not eat or drink,
All my brain is sore with thinking
　　Yet I cannot think.

I have whispered to my pear tree,
　　To the sea I did confess:
Half of me is saying "Never!"
　　Half of me cries "Yes!"

I have such a need of loving:
　　I could burn the night away
With the fire of my longing,
　　Till it died to-day.

O my husband! O my lover!
　　You, I think, are very near:
I am so alight with hoping,
　　So much chilled with fear.

I am seventeen, and they have given
　　Me unto a man of twenty-nine.
He is very strong and lovely;
　　He is mine.

Moon of my young years, forgive me!
　　Good-bye, pear tree! Good-bye, sea!
I am going, going, going,
　　Far from land or sea.

L. A. G. Strong
(1896–)

THE SEALS

LEAVE her alone,
She is the Island's daughter.
Sleek heads, dark heads
Are risen from the water:
Leave her the company
Her songs have brought her.

The old gray music doctors
Of the ocean,
Their holy, happy eyes
Shining devotion,
Applaud and blow
In foam and soft commotion.

It is her hour,
The Island's only daughter.
The dark, sleek heads
Are risen from the water:
Leave her the company
Her songs have brought her.

L. A. G. Strong

ON LOCH MOIDART

You are a sail upon dark landlocked waters,
  A white astonishment to land and sea,
A wavering wonder, fairest of the daughters
  Of tall Aurora in captivity.

No bird, no light, no cloud so cleanly passes
  Over that space between the sea and sky;
No shadow of a gull upon the grasses,
  No proud, plumed star that warns a queen
    to die.

What hill-born wind, to happy fate allied,
  Brought you, O sweet survivor, to my breast,
Wherein becalmed you bid the enchanted tide
  Mirror your silent beauty, and be blest?

Muriel Stuart
(Living)

THE SEED SHOP

HERE in a quiet and dusty room they lie,
  Faded as crumbled stone or shifting sand,
Forlorn as ashes, shrivelled, scentless, dry—
  Meadows and gardens running through my
    hand.

In this brown husk a dale of hawthorn dreams;
 A cedar in this narrow cell is thrust
That will drink deeply of a century's streams;
 These lilies shall make summer on my dust.

Here in their safe and simple house of death,
 Sealed in their shells, a million roses leap;
Here I can blow a garden with my breath,
 And in my hand a forest lies asleep.

REVENANT

" It is cold in the room . . . lamp's out, the
 moon is late.
Something cried out just now as in great
 fear . . .
Ghost that I loved, what brings you suddenly
 near ? "
" *You said you would come to me if I would wait* . . ."
" But you died long ago, poor foolish dear !

And dead and living cannot mix or meet,
You to the dark, and I to love must go. . . ."
" *Last night, but not to-night* . . ." " What can
 you do
To hinder me from one who is as sweet
As you were once ? You're dead ! " " *But
 you're dead, too.*"

Arthur Symons
(1865–1945)

NEAR TINTAGEL

THERE is an austere magic in the place,
A beauty made of some fierce energy
That wars in the black rocks and the wild sea ;
Here land and sea stand grappling, face to face,
Under the canopy of quiet space,
And the land yields, inch by inch, sullenly ;
And day by day the sharp-toothed enemy
Leaps higher and gnaws deeper at its base.

Sunlight and wind bring glories, and the night
Brings splendour, and the dawn a miracle ;
But more than these I have loved an hour of shy
Unfolding twilight, one grey heaven of light
Stripping off splendour to leave visible
The naked majesty of sea and sky.

SONG

I HEAR two voices in the air,
    My soul's voice and my body's voice ;
One bids " remember " : I despair ;
    And one " forget," and I rejoice.

It is the beast in me that makes
Its pasture of the earth and slakes
  A satiable thirst in light.
Why must the man in me convey
Unto the memory of day
  Fear and foreknowledge of the night?

Rachel Annand Taylor
(1876–   )

THE PRINCESS OF SCOTLAND

" WHO are you that so strangely woke,
  And raised a fine hand?"
Poverty wears a scarlet cloke
  In my land.

" Duchies in dreamland, emerald, rose,
  Lie at your command?"
Poverty like a princess goes
  In my land.

" Wherefore the mask of silken lace
  Tied with a golden band?"
Poverty walks with a wanton grace
  In my land.

[241]   Q

" Why do you softly, richly speak
     Rhythm so sweetly-scanned ? "
Poverty hath the Gaelic and Greek
     In my land.

" There's a far-off scent about you seems
     Born in Samarkand."
Poverty hath luxurious dreams
     In my land.

" You have wounds that like passion-flowers
     you hide :
I cannot understand."
Poverty hath one name with Pride
     In my land.

" Oh ! will you draw your last sad breath
     'Mid bitter bent and sand ? "
Poverty begs from none but Death
     In my land.

THE PREFERENCE

" I WILL give you a gay blue cloak
     Soft with queen's miniver."
" He will give me a shroud of flame
     And I find it lovelier."

[242]

"I will lap you in smooth white silk
    In a carved-angel bed."
"But he has doomed me to the stake,
    And I have bowed my head."

THE END OF THE DUEL

THERE'S an end to the duel long fought in the
        Dark,
    In the dangerous moonlighted Past.
Monseigneur my God, a chivalrous lady
    Surrenders at last.

Idly magnanimous, tolerant, intolerant
    Of cowards, frank, fierce, Florentine—
Monseigneur my God, a chivalrous lady
    Thou alone canst divine.

If I be defeated, 'tis by the inviolate
    Stroke of Thy mystical Lance.
Monseigneur my God, a chivalrous lady
    Bemoans not her chance.

If I be unvizored, I gaze at my victor
    With smiling and reconciled eyes.
Monseigneur my God, play fair by the lady—
    Unhelm ere she dies.

[243]

A. S. J. Tessimond
(1902–)

AFTER ATTEMPTED ESCAPE FROM LOVE
(To J. M.)

HE who has once been caught in a silver chain
    may burn and toss and fret.
He will never be bound with bronze again;
    he will not be forgiven; will never forget.
He who has looked at the golden grapes of the sun
    will call no sour fruit sweet.
He will turn from the moon's green apples and run,
    though they fall in his hand, though they
    lie at his feet.

SECOND PORTRAIT OF J. M.

SHE has stood upon the rims of many worlds
    And looked at many voids with open eyes
And turned back smiling and returned unscathed,
    Remaining young and wise.

She has drunk the sun, embraced the air, spun
    Earth
    Upon her fingertips, and laughed and cried
A lifetime in a day, but never yet
    Been wholly satisfied.

She is armoured, confident, complete, exultant,
  Born to command, star-destined to success—
And yet, a little, longs to rest, disarmed,
  Tired of tirelessness.

Edward Thomas
(1878–1917)

THE LANE

SOME day, I think there will be people enough
In Froxfield to pick all the blackberries
Out of the hedges of Green Lane, the straight
Broad lane where now September hides herself
In bracken and blackberry, harebell and dwarf
      gorse.
To-day, where yesterday a hundred sheep
Were nibbling, halcyon bells shake to the sway
Of waters that no vessel ever sailed . . .
  It is a kind of spring : the chaffinch tries
His song. For heat it is like summer too.
This might be winter's quiet. While the glint
Of hollies dark in the swollen hedges lasts—
One mile—and those bells ring, little I know
Or heed if time be still the same, until
The lane ends and once more all is the same.

Edward Thomas

THE WATCHERS

By the Ford at the town's edge
Horse and carter rest:
The carter smokes on the bridge
Watching the water press in swathes about his
    horse's chest.

From the inn one watches, too,
In the room for visitors
That has no fire, but a view
And many cases of stuffed fish, vermin, and
    kingfishers.

Francis Thompson
(1859–1907)

AN ARAB LOVE-SONG

THE hunchèd camels of the night*
Trouble the bright
And silver waters of the moon.
The maiden of the Morn will soon
Through Heaven stray and sing,
Star gathering.

    * Cloud-shapes observed by travellers in the East.

[246]

Now while the dark about our loves is strewn,
Light of my dark, blood of my heart, Oh, come!
And night will catch her breath up, and be dumb.

Leave thy father, leave thy mother
And thy brother;
Leave the black tents of thy tribe apart!
Am I not thy father and thy brother,
And thy mother?
And thou—what needest with thy tribe's black
    tents
Who hast the red pavilion of my heart?

TO A SNOWFLAKE

WHAT heart could have thought you?—
Past our devisal
(O filigree petal!)
Fashioned so purely,
Fragilely, surely,
From what Paradisal
Imagineless metal,
Too costly for cost?
Who hammered you, wrought you,
From argentine vapour?—
" God was my shaper.

Passing surmisal,
He hammered, He wrought me,
From curled silver vapour,
To lust of His mind :—
Thou could'st not have thought me !
So purely, so palely,
Tinily, surely,
Mightily, frailly,
Insculped and embossed,
With His hammer of wind,
And His graver of frost."

IN NO STRANGE LAND

O WORLD invisible, we view thee,
　　O world intangible, we touch thee,
O world unknowable, we know thee,
　　Inapprehensible, we clutch thee !

Does the fish soar to find the ocean,
　　The eagle plunge to find the air—
That we ask of the stars in motion
　　If they have rumour of thee there ?

Not where the wheeling systems darken,
　　And our benumbed conceiving soars !—
The drift of pinions, would we hearken,
　　Beats at our own clay-shuttered doors.

Francis Thompson

The angels keep their ancient places ;—
    Turn but a stone, and start a wing !
'Tis ye, 'tis your estrangèd faces,
    That miss the many-splendoured thing.

But (when so sad thou canst not sadder)
    Cry ;—and upon thy so sore loss
Shall shine the traffic of Jacob's ladder
    Pitched betwixt Heaven and Charing Cross.

Yea, in the night, my Soul, my daughter,
    Cry,—clinging Heaven by the hems ;
And lo, Christ walking on the water
    Not of Gennesareth, but Thames !

Wilfrid Thorley
(1878–   )

CHANT FOR REAPERS

Why do you hide, O dryads ! when we seek
Your healing hands in solace ?
Who shall soften like you the places rough ?
Who shall hasten the harvest ?

Why do you fly, O dryads ! when we pray
For laden boughs and blossom ?
Who shall quicken like you the sapling trees ?
Who shall ripen the orchards ?

[249]

Bare in the wind the branches wave and break.
The hazel nuts are hollow.
Who shall garner the wheat if you be gone?
Who shall sharpen his sickle?

Wine have we spilt, O dryads! on our knees
Have made you our oblation.
Who shall save us from dearth if you be fled?
Who shall comfort and kindle?

Sadly we delve the furrows, string the vine
Whose flimsy burden topples.
Downward tumble the woods if you be dumb,
Stript of honey and garland.

Why do you hide, O dryads! when we call,
With pleading hands uplifted?
Smile and bless us again that all be well;
Smile again on your children.

THE WEATHER-VANE

O Steeple-cock, stoop down to me
    And tell me what you see afar!
A sail that flickers on the sea
    No bigger than a star.

[250]

Wilfrid Thorley

O make your fledge a beacon, fowl,
  And let your wings be lanterns both !
Afar I see the tempest scowl,
  And all the waves are wroth.

Look well again, good steeple-cock,
  And can you see her lantern-spark ?
Nay, now she runs upon a rock,
  And founders in the dark.

O steeple-cock, say one is saved,
  One only lad that shall not drown !
I saw a sudden hand that waved
  But once, and then went down.

Fly, steeple-cock, with my true pledge,
  And say I love him, ere he die !
Too heavy is my golden fledge,
  Good lass ! I cannot fly.

Pamela Travers
(1904–   )

THE DARK HEART

THE equinoxes pass
  With banners and are gone ;
She sits among the seasons
  Stiller than stone

Immutable and bowed
  Beneath the wheeling spheres—
Lord, how can you get in
  That dark heart of hers

That has for its business
  The root and the seed?
From these she will not stir
  Nor lift her head

For angel, prince or power,
  Nor you—but oh, disguise!
And when black boughs break out
  In stars before her eyes

Go in with them, go in
  With summer to her thought;
Fly to her ear upon
  The cuckoo's double note;

Be the wild sloe, no fruit
  Ripened but found her,
Hid in the brown creek water
  You may surround her;

Press through the heifer's flank
  Where her cheek bends,
Run in the jets of milk
  Down through her hands;

And when the evening tides
   Brim up and to her stream
Her naked lover goes,
   Lord, go thou in with him!

WATER AND STONE

BORN of water, born of water
The sea's child, the river's daughter,
She must find a man of stone
Adamantine and alone,

Who breaking through her pliant side
Withstands the onslaught of her tide,
And though heart, mind and sense be gone
Down in her waters, will not drown.

Naked he within her stream
And naked she encircling him
Must battle give and may not cease
Till rock have motion, water peace;

And those great foemen in one bed
Measure the dark and are afraid
No more of love, nor time, nor death:
So, mixing deep breath with light breath,

Each knowing and to other known,
They fuse together sea and stone
And of their single essence build
As once in Judah that bright child.

FAREWELL AND HAIL

Now the planets wheel away
Leaf and sap to root are gone,
So unto his elements
Let him return
That was a burning-glass
Glowing between
Darkness and light, that drew
Sun down to stone.

The self-renewing phœnix fire
Of mind be loosed and spirit's air !
Loose earth and waters deep that made
The body's ore !
When in the frosty firmament
Such elements again cohere
Shall not the watching Magi see
Not man but star ?

Altair, Vega, Cassiopiea,
Sister Pleiads, Columbæ,
Betelgeux, Aldebaran,
Now receive a man set free ;

Free of the brother opposites,
Pole and tropic, false and true,
Centre and circumference,
The moon's tidal ebb and flow!

Beyond the beat of earth, beyond
The power of sequent night and day
The happy lover's free of love
And time, love's sole alloy,
Free of all that's measured by
The double sigh of mortal breath,
Free—ultimate enfranchisement—
Free of death.

Berenice Golden-hair,
Cor Hydræ, the lonely one,
Capella, Arcturus, Orion,
Behold your dear companion!

W. J. Turner
(1889–1946)

FRITILLARY

FAR-AWAY, forlorn—forlorn, far away!
The fountain in the garden, the moon in the
    sky—
A wind dies down, stirs, turning with a sigh

Under the solitary tree : melancholy the *Day*
Throws her dark cloak in the pool and steals
    away
Her nakedness reflected on the hills. Now lie
Her evening diamonds in the water. Passing by
A wandering fritillary is her perfume grey.
Night and the frenzy of the stars festooning the
    tree,
The crackle of the brilliant water cutting the
    hill—
Far-away, forlorn ! This is not the place,
This is not what we were seeking, nor that
    epiphany
That shall come suddenly, when it is all still,
When there is nothing but myself and I face to
    face.

Evelyn Underhill

(1875–1941)

THE LADY POVERTY

I MET her on the Umbrian hills,
    Her hair unbound, her feet unshod :
As one whom secret glory fills
    She walked, alone with God.

Evelyn Underhill

I met her in the city street:
   Oh, changed was all her aspect then!
With heavy eyes and weary feet
   She walked alone, with men.

Sherard Vines
(1890–   )

DAY BY THE DESERT

ALONG the dry coast of Arabia
I heard the quail and the hard rattling tide.
Distant, as untuned bells by a mere-side,
Gaunt palm-fronds clanked, troubling the rare
And bitter morning air.
Then Azrael called to Ithuriel
Flashing his brass wings yellower than sand;
Ithuriel with a golden horn replied.
Out of the resonant land
Noon passed and evening died.

E. H. Visiak
(1878–   )

THE SLUM CHILD

I'M going to the seaside, to lovely Herne Bay.
   Ho! what a beano.

I'm going with the school treat on the second
of May.
>> Shan't I be glad!

I dreamt that the sands was a frothing gold
cup.
>> Ho! what a beano.
And a scorching great cat came and drank it
all up.
>> Wasn't I mad!

I'll see the great green waves come rolling to
shore.
>> Ho! what a beano.
And Father and Mother can't clout me no
more.
>> Shan't I be glad!

I'll go for a long, lovely bathe in the sea.
>> Ho! what a beano.
They'll look and they'll look, but they'll never
find me.
>> Won't they be mad!

Charles Weekes
(1867–1946)

THINK

THINK, the raggëd turf-boy urges
O'er the dusty road his asses;
Think, on the sea-shore far the lonely
Heron wings along the sand;
Think, in woodland under oak-boughs
Now the streaming sunbeam passes;
And bethink thee thou art servant
To the same all-moving hand.

TITAN

WHAT matters where the great God flings
    Down on earth's floor thy thinking clay,
    If thou canst rise and live to-day
The life of emperors and kings!

So take thy soul and keep it sane;
    And, treading firm the green earth-sod,
    Look upwards from that place to God,
That He may see thy soul again,

There undejected, there unhurled
    Asunder—sick with mortal change:
    Self-held from star to star to range,
Or one with all the working world.

O King of kings and emperors !
    Though vagabond of night and morn :
    Some dusty quarry-fellow born
To walk beside a tattered horse.

IN THE PARK

She ne'er shall be made of the throng of wives :
    Her body is brown—as the golden dun
    Of the honey-bees in the evening sun,
When they come singing home to the quiet
    hives :
She sits, where the green water spurts and drives,
    On the ledge of the monster marble dish,
    Playing a game with the silly fish,
To bereave them of their lives.

THE REBUKE

I will not understand your voice.
    Look on my breasts—my face—my hair :
These things are mine. There is no noise
    Within this flesh of your despair.
These are my weapons, these my wine
    With which I make men blind and drunk :
I, Circe, know the snouted swine :
    I, Judith, laugh, and roll the trunk

Of Holofernes from the bed :
   And if the accusing eye-balls stare
Or the lips blame me of the dead—
   Holding the skull up by the hair,
Upon the mouth I strike the dog
   Who knows not, choosing his own game :
He wins ?—I lie there like a log :
   He loses ?—he shall do the same !
—Ah, if you plunder all my pride
   How poor you make me in the end !
If God be surely on your side,
   Leave me, at least, the Deuce, my friend !

THE IDLER

I move through the idle street,
   Nearer your happy place ;
But I see in the idle, strange faces I meet,
   Only one face.

And day-long I stand above
   My tired and idle loom ;
For between your face and mine, love,
   Is the world's room.

IN BRITTANY

In Brittany I loſt my way :
　　Ah, happy girl-child of sixteen,
　　Whatever my ſtrange tongue might mean
You knew not, nor the thing to say,

Till a mad kiss fell on your lips,
　　When, unconfused, you ceased to smile, ·
　　And answered : " Up the hill a mile
Stands fair ' Our Lady of the Ships ' :

" We pray there for our folk at sea
　　And then they are not wrecked nor tossed,
　　But come back safe and are not loſt—
And you may pray there, sir, for me."

Dorothy Wellesley
(Duchess of Wellington)

(1889–　　)

FROM "MATRIX"

The spiritual, the carnal, are one.
For when love is greatly found,
It outcries, as men cry
When in pain to be laid on the ground ;
As men in pain moan for the grave ;

Hear : how in love the lips moan,
For Man must pursue
Love the lamp back to darkness again ;
Is not this death too ?

.   .   .   .

Earth, back to the earth.

Out of her beauty at birth,
Out of her I came
To lose all that I knew :
Though somehow at birth I died,
One night she will teach me anew :
Peace ? The same,
As a woman's, a mother's
Breast undenied, to console
The small bones built in the womb,
The womb that loathed the bones,
And cast out the soul.

Anna Wickham

(1884–1947)

MARE BRED FROM PEGASUS

For God's sake, stand off from me :
There's a brood mare here going to kick like hell
With a mad up-rising energy ;
And where the wreck will end who'll tell ?

She'll splinter the stable and eat a groom.
For God's sake, give me room;
Give my will room.

"Make Beauty for me!"—that was what you said,
While I was cowering at your dying fire,
Laconic, blowing at your chill desire.
Then flame broke out in me to char you dead;
A fierce hope and a more fierce distrust
To char your bones to dust.

My pretty jockey, you've the weight
To be a rider, but not my mate;
And yet your spirit's bold to impregnate,
And I'm a lashing, butting hate.

Since my poor life began
I had desire to serve my man
With all my wit, all imagination,
And every subtle beauty of creation;
And you come late
And mock me in my masterless hard state.

"Make Beauty for me!"—that was what you said.
Desire rose up in me to strike you dead,
With that mad mare my will
To lash and smash her fill.

Run, run, and hide you in some woman's heart,
In a retreat I cannot kick apart!

SONG OF OPHELIA THE SURVIVOR

THERE is no smirch of sin in you, only its fires.
You are a man burned white with merciless
    desires;
A restless heat consumes you, and your brain,
Tortured to torturing, craves for ugly pain.

Beauty still lives in you, and from her seat
Controls your glances, and directs your feet;
One look from you taught me so much of love,
I have all pleasure, just to watch you move.

That look was like a wet blue mist of flowers,
Which held compelling loveliness and sleepy
    powers.
I dreamed of calling pipes down a warm glade;
By the transposéd music of your soul I was
    betrayed.

Pipe for me, my dear lover! I will come,
And your sick soul shall find in me a home;
I will be your house, clean, high, and strong.
And you shall live in me, all winter long.

As you are fevered, I will be a pool,
Full of green shadows, level, silent, cool.
You shall bathe in me, in my being move;
I will put out your fires with my strong love.

CONSCIENCE

(Written for Fytton Armstrong)

I DREAMED my heart was a grave
In which were dead embalmed princesses,
In jewelled stomachers and dresses,
Flaunting their never-rotting tresses
For the skull smile of the brave.

I dreamed Dionysius spoke:
A free beast howled from the Christians'
    heaven;
All ugly cerements were riven;
And breath, and blood, and breasts were given;
And the kings and the girls awoke.

GARNETT'S GARDEN

I LOOK down from my window,
And I see
A ramble of forget-me-not
Beneath a flowery tree;

As if the sky had fallen
To let pass
A lovely girl
To dance upon the grass.
I could lie happy dead beneath your garden
If my soul could walk the skies
With such white lovely women,
In a cool paradise.

AMENDE
(Of J. G.)

THIS courtly boy who brings me books
Is agate in my childhood's brooks.
He is a fawn, and a fine lawn—
Two lawns, woven and growing.
He's like a subtle play on words,
And like the swelling throats of birds
Which—by their showing—
Give promise of dear life to be,
Pleasure and peace and harmony.

THE POET

HERE is he, at this moment, which is Time's end,
Lonely as he was born, without a friend.
And he has called the hungry to his door,
And he has shared his bounty with the poor.

He has been feasted, he has been desired;
Lovers have drunk of him, till they were tired.
All men have ate his councils and passed by,
Thankless, as who shall thank the sky.

Margaret L. Woods
(1856–1945)

TO THE FORGOTTEN DEAD

To the forgotten dead,
Come, let us drink in silence ere we part.
To every fervent yet resolvèd heart
That brought its tameless passion and its tears,
Renunciation and laborious years,
To lay the deep foundations of our race,
To rear its mighty ramparts overhead
And light its pinnacles with golden grace,
To the unhonoured dead.

To the forgotten dead,
Whose dauntless hands were stretched to grasp
the rein
Of Fate and hurl into the void again
Her thunder-hoofèd horses, rushing blind
Earthward along the courses of the wind.

Among the stars, along the wind in vain
Their souls were scattered and their blood was
    shed,
And nothing, nothing of them doth remain.
            To the thrice-perished dead.

GENIUS LOCI

PEACE, Shepherd, peace ! What boots it singing
    on ?
Since long ago grace-giving Phœbus died,
And all the train that loved the stream-bright side
Of the poetic mount with him are gone
Beyond the shores of Styx and Acheron,
In unexplorèd realms of night to hide.
The clouds that strew their shadows far and wide
Are all of Heaven that visits Helicon.

Yet here, where never muse or god did haunt,
Still may some nameless power of Nature stray,
Pleased with the reedy stream's continual chant
And purple pomp of these broad fields in May.
The shepherds meet him where he herds the
    kine,
And careless pass him by whose is the gift
    divine.

Theodore Wratislaw
(1871–1933)

INSCRIPTION
(To Selwyn Image)

IF, passer-by, who idly stand and read,
If thou bereft of love shouldst haply lead
Thy sorrow through these old forgotten graves

And deem that I sleep well who lie beneath
These withered flowers and faded ivy wreath,
Without the soul that aches, the heart that
    craves,

Be glad, O traveller, of thy happy hours!
Thou hast the sunlight and renascent flowers,
And life is sweet and time may bring delight;

But I must yearn among the silent dead
For even the life of grasses on my head,
So sad it is, the shadow of the night.

AT NIGHT

IN the wild heaven the wan moon weeps
    From eyelids fringed with drifting cloud,
And on the pebbles inward sweeps
    The tide and moans aloud.

The face of night is seared and blind,
  The rough sea cannot sleep ;
Weep all thy tears, O rain-drenched wind,
  For one who may not weep !

Andrew Young
(1885–   )

LATE AUTUMN

The boy called to his team
  And with blue-glancing share
Turned up the rape and turnip
  With yellow charlock to spare.

The long lean thistles stood
  Like beggars ragged and blind,
Half their white silken locks
  Blown away in the wind.

But I thought not once of winter
  Or summer that was past
Till I saw that slant-legged robin
  With autumn on his chest.

Ella Young
(Living)

THE ROSE OF SILENCE

In a green stillness hidden from sun and moon
        Under the sea,
A blossom swings by the High-Queen's doon
        On a silver tree;
And every poet has dreamed since time begun
        Of that hidden place,
But only those who have said farewell to the sun
    May come to the doon by the silver tree
Or find in hollow or height,
    Under the still green tideless sea
The Rose of Silence and Night.

Index

[**273**]

S

Index

Index

Index

[276]

Index

Index

[279]

Index

Index

[281]

Index

[282]

Index

TALES OF HORROR AND THE SUPERNATURAL

By Arthur Machen

ARTHUR MACHEN HAS LONG BEEN RECOGNISED AS one of the great masters of the horror story and the tale involving the supernatural, but no conventional ghost story ever came from his pen. He was in addition a master of the English language and able to turn worn phrases into bright new word patterns. In this volume the best of Machen's tales are collected, ranging in length from short stories, such as *The Bowmen* and *N*, to short novels such as *The Terror* and *The Great God Pan*. This latter, originally published in John Lane's Keynotes Series, has already become an established classic in the great Gothic tradition of Horace Walpole and the Brontes. The volume contains a long and interesting critical introduction by Philip Van Doren Stern, and a portrait in collotype of the author.

Demy 8vo.   480 pp.   21s. net

THE GREEN CARNATION

By Robert Hichens

WHEN "THE GREEN CARNATION" MADE ITS FIRST appearance anonymously in 1895 it quickly became a social topic, much speculation being aroused as to the identity of its author. Its immediate success can be attributed to the fact that it not only provided a most amusing skit on the so-called Æsthetic Movement, but also introduced into its pages easily recognisable portraits of Oscar Wilde, the high priest of the cult, and the young, good-looking and aristocratic Lord Alfred Douglas. For many years Mr. Hichens, whose first essay in fiction it was, has declined to allow the book to be reprinted and, well known by reputation as it is, to most readers to-day it can be little more than a name. It now makes its reappearance for the first time after a lapse of over forty years, the author adding an Introduction in which he tells us how the book came to be written and narrates the circumstances in which he came into contact with its protagonists. No alteration whatever has been made in the text of the book as it was originally printed.

Crown 8vo.   8s. 6d. net

THE RETURN OF THE PRODIGAL

By St. John Hankin

St. John Emile Clavering Hankin terminated his life abruptly before he reached the age of forty years, at the plenitude of his powers as a dramatist in the tradition of Congreve, Sheridan and Wilde. At his death his "theatre" comprised two short one-act plays, four complete plays, and one unfinished play, afterwards completed by George Calderon. It is useless to speculate what further contribution he might have made to the contemporary theatre had his life run its normal course, but it is relevant to quote Bernard Shaw's emphatic statement: "All Hankin's plays are remarkably equal in merits; he has no failures". *The Return of the Prodigal* was originally produced in London in 1905 under the direction of Granville Barker, and Mr. John Gielgud's recent revival of the play which, like all Hankin's other plays, has been out of print for many years, has prompted this new edition, for which Mr. St. John Ervine provides a long and interesting Introduction.

Cr. 8vo.   Cloth, 6s., Paper 4s. net

THE BEST IN THEIR KIND: FIFTY-TWO ENGLISH AUTHORS

By S. P. B. MAIS

MR. MAIS' REPUTATION FOR AROUSING ENTHUSIASM for the great authors in the minds of several generations of boys and girls is well known. Here is the harvest of his life-long reading, a selection from the works of fifty-two authors who have made a deep impression on him, together with their life-stories, showing how their environment and circumstances influenced their outlook and their literary genius.

Demy 8vo.   500 pp.   21s. net